I WALK AND TALK WITH ANGELS

I WALK
AND TALK
WITH ANGELS
A True Life Story

Edward W. Oldring

Exposition Press   *Hicksville, New York*

First Edition

© 1978 by Edward W. Oldring

ISBN 0-682-49067-9

Printed in the United States of America

This book is gratefully and lovingly dedicated
to
my wife,
Patricia Joy Warren Oldring,
my wisest counselor,
my severest critic,
my truest friend

CONTENTS

PREFACE

The events I have described in this book are all true. I have described them as accurately as possible. The conversations I have reported both between myself and two of God's angels and between myself and the people mentioned in the book are also true and as accurate as I am able to make them, which I believe is extremely accurate.

Many people have read the manuscript of this book. Some have expressed the opinion that one or two events should be deleted. I have not recorded everything that happened in my encounter with God through two of His angels. It is possible that some of these experiences will be recorded in a book soon to follow. Everything reported in this book did happen, and as I have sought to keep faith with God and report only what has taken place and record it exactly as it did take place, I feel I must pass my experience on to all who wish to read it.

Some suggested that the real names of people mentioned should be changed. I have acted upon this advice. Thus, some people are identified only by a letter of the alphabet or by names I have simply borrowed in order that no one be embarrassed or inconvenienced because of this book. The names of many of my true friends mentioned are their real names.

ACKNOWLEDGMENTS

I wish to acknowledge the genuine love and support of my family—first, my wife, Patricia Joy; second, my sons and daughters: Edward Robin Oldring, now Reverend Robin Oldring and his wife, Bonnie; Brian Warren Oldring, now Dr. Brian Oldring, and his wife, Jane; Margaret Ann Smeaton, my only daughter, and her husband, Dr. Melvin Douglas Smeaton; my son, John Alan Oldring, and his wife, Bonnie; and my son, David Rodney Oldring, still living at home but with plans of his own for the near future.

My wife and I wish to thank our many friends for simply being true friends and encouragers. They know who they are—and so do we. A special thanks to those friends whose financial assistance made this book possible.

I WALK AND TALK WITH ANGELS

I

I WALK WITH ANGELS

As I reached for my telephone in my spacious office in Gaetz Memorial United Church in the city of Red Deer, in the heart of the province of Alberta, Canada, I automatically glanced at the clock on the wall. It was twenty-two minutes to five.

"Good afternoon, Ed Oldring speaking."

"Mr. Oldring, this is the children's ward at the General Hospital . . . ah . . . we have a baby girl . . . we don't think she will live through the night . . . her parents would like you to come to the hospital and baptize the baby."

"Are the parents there now?"

"Mrs. B. is here; Mr. B. will be here a little before six o'clock."

I knew the parents; they were not members of our congregation, but they often attended and I had served the family on a number of occasions.

"Would you like me to come right away?" I inquired.

"The mother would prefer that you come just before six when

15

both she and the father are here. Dr. Williams is going to perform a tracheotomy shortly before six."

"Please tell Mrs. B. I'll be there and do everything I can."

As I walked from the parking lot of the hospital toward the main entrance, Dr. Y., a throat specialist, joined me. We had gone to high school together.

"Where are you going, Ed?"

"To Pediatrics."

"So am I, let's take the elevator."

As we entered the ward, Dr. Bill (that is the name I always used for Dr. Williams), and the anesthetist were already there. As it turned out, Dr. Y. was going to assist in the same operation. The four of us spoke together briefly as a nurse brought a surgical gown for me and helped me into it. Without a moment's pause she beckoned me to the room where the baby and her parents were.

"Take as much time as you need, don't rush," Dr. Bill said as I walked toward the room.

The baby was twenty-two months old, in an oxygen tent and fighting for every breath. My heart went out not only to the tiny little life struggling so desperately in what surely looked like a battle without hope, but to the young parents also as they stood by so silently and so helplessly.

We talked for just a moment, then I turned to the nurse and asked, "Do you mind if I open this flap?" The oxygen tent was securely sealed, but there were zippered flaps on both sides.

"Not at all," she said, reaching out and opening it for me. I could now place my hand on the baby's head and did so as I administered the Sacrament of Holy Baptism. When the Sacrament was completed, I asked the parents to place their hands on mine as my hand continued to rest gently on the baby's head. Then I said an additional prayer—a very simple prayer. I asked God to take this child into His care and keep her in His love and His mercy, and in His great wisdom to send what was best into this child's life. We then withdrew our hands and zipped up the flap on the tent.

Immediately an amazing thing began to happen. The baby girl began to move her head and arms with a new freedom. She was clearly indicating that she wanted the oxygen tent removed. She looked around for her parents. I leaned over the bed and the child looked into my eyes and smiled. Then the baby sat up. Dr. Bill came in and removed the tent. The baby was very active and all signs of distress had disappeared. The baby was healed. Dr. Bill examined the baby carefully, then he left the room. He was back in an instant with the two other doctors and a second examination was made. The baby girl was becoming impatient; she wanted out of bed. There was no mistake—the baby was healed.

The doctors moved from the room to the hallway. I followed and heard Dr. Y. and Dr. H. "rib" Dr. Bill about his inability to make a diagnosis. He turned toward them and he was smiling. He said, "Haven't you ever heard of a spiritual healing?"

I returned to speak with the parents. They were, of course, grateful, surprised, speechless, but obviously humbly grateful.

Later at home, as I recounted the events of this evening for my wife, Joy, I said, "It wasn't anything that I did. I simply prayed to God. He healed the baby."

In the weeks that followed I didn't dwell greatly on this event. I told one or two of my associates of the healing. I did not, however, read anything into it. I had offered a prayer, and God in His infinite wisdom and goodness had given more than had been asked. This was not surprising. There were, however, to be surprises and this event turned out to be one part of a new beginning.

About two months later something happened that left no doubt about a new beginning. I was sitting in our living room in my favorite chair, a reclining rocker that my wife, Joy, had bought for me. I got up to walk down the hallway in our home.

Suddenly my feet became heavy and my step ponderous. Then my stride changed. In a flash I knew that someone was walking with me. I was elated, but at that moment the elation was all within. In the days that followed, wherever I went someone walked with me. My stride continued to be changed. It lengthened; it shortened; it quickened; it slowed down again. Something new was happening in my life and my ministry.

Now my mind did dwell upon this "something new," and I made an astonishing discovery—it was not new at all. My mind began to reach back—at first to my second pastoral charge after ordination. Several things had happened in our five and one-half years on that pastoral charge. For instance, some of the sermons that I prepared and delivered seemed to "come into my mind." This became such a vivid process that one Sunday morning I told the congregation that I could not really call the sermon they were about to hear "my sermon."

"You see," I told them, "as I sat in the study this past week thinking what I should say to you this morning, I got the distinct feeling that someone was standing behind me telling me what to say."

This process became so real to me that I thought about it a great deal. It did not happen all the time. And again, I did not read too much into it, although I thought about it often. God's time had not yet come.

Other memorable things happened. For instance, I was called to the hospital to the room of a very pretty young wife and mother. She was seriously ill and at that moment in a seizure that shook her whole body. Her husband was there, so were her mother and father, her sister and another friend of the family, a young man. All those in the room were gripped by the seriousness and the anguish of watching this young woman with whom they could not communicate. The mother asked me to offer a prayer. I laid my hand on the forehead of the woman and in a very simple manner asked God, in His loving kindness, to grant this, His child, peace. Peace came instantly. The seizure left, calm returned and the patient sank gently into a peace-filled sleep. In the hallway a moment later her husband threw his head upon my shoulder and wept without shame.

A day or so later I met the young man who had been in the room that day. He was not a member of a church; he was not a man who was active in worship. He had obviously been touched and he was in a reflective mood. He said to me, "It must be wonderful to be able to help people like that."

I was not, however, the source of help—and I knew it. It was not I who granted peace that day; it was God. Thus I did not tell anyone about this incident, nor did I consider it unusual in any way. I had offered a prayer—God had answered it. That to me was not a surprise. God, by then, had answered many prayers in my life. Not all of them were answered instantly. One of my most cherished prayers was not answered for nearly ten years. When the answer finally came, it was beautiful beyond my wildest expectations. God's time and God's timing is of the utmost importance. At this point it had not entered my mind that God might be holding forth to me one of His greatest gifts— the gift of healing.

Surprises were to come and in great abundance. For now, someone was walking with me. It was "something new," but I could look back and see that it was really not new at all.

I looked back again to a day near the end of my final year in theology. I was not only taking a full course in theology but at the same time serving a pastoral charge made up of three villages. There was a full preaching service at each point every Sunday. The distance from the college was one hundred and eleven miles; the distance around the pastoral charge was seventy-five miles. It was a heavy load and at times it was difficult to keep up with all the demands from what should have been two full-time jobs. Finally the Saturday came when I was totally unprepared for services on Sunday. Our principal had told us that this would happen to every one of us at least once. He told us, "If you find yourself on a Saturday evening with nothing prepared for

Sunday, don't stay up half the night trying to put something together. Go to bed, get a good night's rest, then get up early in the morning. You will find you are not only more able to prepare for the day ahead, but more likely to do a good job if you are not tired out."

I remembered and took his advice. I went to bed and, as usual, slept well. Toward morning a beautiful experience came over me. A sermon began to present itself to my mind. I relaxed and listened to a good sermon, then woke up and wrote it down. I was not the only one who thought it was a good sermon; on all three preaching points people offered special commendation.

The only person, before now, to whom I had told this experience was my wife. She listened with interest but made no comment. Neither she nor I ever mentioned it again, although from the day it happened until now, I have often pondered it in my mind. Today I understand it. My whole life through I have walked with two of God's angels.

II

I TALK WITH ANGELS

Something new was happening in my life, all right, and yet it was not new. I could look back over the years and see that there had always been a presence with me. In fact, before too long I was to look back as far as my early childhood and read clear and unmistakable proof of this presence. Before too long I was to learn that two of God's angels were walking with me now and had been walking with me my whole life through.

Things began to happen fast—astonishing things, beautiful things. I found my head moving without my willing it or causing it. Sometimes it would move downward as if to say "yes"; sometimes it would move from side to side as if to say "no." By now I was expecting the unusual and in a way instinctively understanding and responding. I began to ask questions—hundreds of them—and my head would nod "yes" or "no." There were many chances to verify these answers. I will tell you some of these later. For now let me say this: the day soon came when a voice spoke into my ear in clear, concise English, saying, "We are God's angels."

"We!" I replied instinctively.

"Yes, there are two of us. We are servants of God and He has appointed us to walk with you. We were at your birth; we have been with you through your entire life. We have a lot of surprises in store for you. Don't be afraid; God has a special ministry for you to perform, and we will share in it with you."

For the next few days a great quiet settled over me. I pondered all that had happened and shared it only with my wife. Then a great elation entered my life, and I caught an insight into what it means to be "drunk with the spirit," that is, lifted to such a height of joy that to some it seems like your actions are those of someone under a stimulus beyond normal life. I began to have some small insight into how the disciples felt at Pentecost when they were accused of being drunk, to which charge Peter answered, "No, they are not drunk; after all, it is only nine o'clock in the morning."

From that moment on, along with my normal duties as the senior minister to a large congregation and my responsibilities as a husband and father, I entered into almost continual conversation with two of God's angels. In regard to ministering the two went hand in hand. The angels were now playing a vital role in my ministry. This role has been most significant, but it has changed in some respects over the past few years. There was an added significance to the relationship in those days. I had a great deal to learn, and the teaching-learning experience was all woven in with everything else that was going on. It was a constant and a demanding process.

At this point I was still asking questions, one after another. The angels were asking me questions too—pointed questions, questions that made me examine many aspects of life, especially my life. Most of the time my questions were answered; sometimes the only answer would be, "You will know that in time," or, "That is not your concern."

This preliminary method of communication went on for

about ten weeks. Then one day one of the angels said, "This method is too slow. We are going to teach you a faster way."

In fact, they taught me four methods. Just when we would seem to be getting along fine with a new way of communicating, one of them would say, "We are going to teach you a faster way."

The fourth and final method was introduced with these words, "Ed, we are now going to teach you to talk with us much the same way we communicate in God's eternity."

This method is mind to mind. It is not mental telepathy. Words, phrases, sentences—all are formed and spoken but at great speeds. Yet there is no sense of speed. Words are also interspersed with pictures. These too may come at great speeds, but, again, there is no feeling of haste. There is a simple understanding of what is being said or shown. Today any one of these four methods may be used or any combination of the four.

Mere communication was not the only purpose in the teaching-learning process. Among the many other things that were being taught were these: first, I had to learn to converse with my angles at the same time that I was carrying on a conversation with another person, or with a group of people or while delivering a sermon; and second, to have complete control of my emotions at all times. For instance, I might be experiencing one emotion in a conversation with one of the angels. This emotion had to be controlled if I was experiencing a different emotion in a conversation with people or preaching a sermon. In this and all other areas of the learning process, just when I seemed to be gaining a degree of efficiency the pressures would increase to press me on and on to widen and expand my threshold of ability to perform.

There was much to learn. I had to learn to recognize beyond a doubt when it was one of my angels speaking to me; I had to test every message for accuracy and detect the slightest flaw. At the same time I was compelled to use my own intelligence, my own experience, my own training, my own knowledge of God, of Christ, of the Holy Spirit and of the Scriptures.

While all this was going on other things were happening. My

angels told me their names. They told me a great deal about themselves. They always called me Ed. Most people I know do. The angels nearly always prefixed their statements to me with this name. They told me many things about my life. For instance, one said to me, "Ed, you have been very near to death many times. We have pulled you back from death many times."

I was not aware of this, however, I had no reason to doubt it. Nor was that all; within the next few months my angels were to snatch me back from the jaws of death on at least three more occasions.

Following this announcement it became the custom of my angels to show me in a most fascinating way "flashbacks" of my life. There were many reasons for these flashbacks. First, the angels were letting me know for certain that they had been with me all of my life. Still another reason was to show me actual scenes from times when they caused things to happen. Lastly, they let me see at least some of the times they had saved me from death.

I was a pilot in the Royal Canadian Air Force serving overseas during the Second World War. One day I was flying a twin-engine Beaufighter on a training flight out of Scotland over the North Sea. We sometimes flew at very low altitudes, as low as fifty feet above the water, in order to avoid detection by enemy radar. Suddenly one motor conked out. A Beaufighter is not meant to be flown on one motor. It has been done but it requires great skill and perhaps even something more than that. The likelihood in this circumstance is greater that a Beaufighter would go down rather than up. My plane that day shot up with an astonishing suddenness. I had not done a thing. There wasn't time. I looked at the altimeter and saw that we had risen by 500 feet. I changed the conked motor to an auxiliary tank and brought the plane back to base without further incident. At the time, and as I have pondered it, I thought it was likely that God had caused my plane to rise. I did not say so to anyone; I wasn't sure. It was, however, one of the times my angels had saved my life.

Another event will seem rather trivial, but it has an interesting aspect to it, and I don't suppose that death can ever be viewed as trivial. Joy and I owned a trailer. We loved to spend time together in the peace and relative seclusion of our trailer. One summer night after we had retired we thought we could smell gas from our propane tank. I felt I should investigate. I had grown up in Alberta, where everyone used natural gas. I had often seen a plumber use a match to test a joint for a leak. If there was a leak the gas would simply burn up with a slight puff. I assumed propane would do the same. I therefore set out to find the leak with a match. It was a calm, still night. Yet whenever I tried to touch the match to the joints on the propane tank "a strong wind" would blow the flame away. The match was never blown out. I tried to shelter the match and tried to test the joint from every side. Always "the wind" blew the flame away from the tank. It was exasperating. In the end I took a wrench and tightened every nut I could, and Joy and I slept in peace.

The next morning I was inspecting the propane bottle again, and I told my neighbor I had tried to find a leak with a match the night before. He couldn't believe what he heard. He said, "Whew! Boy, you are lucky that both you and the trailer are here this morning."

I had forgotten the incident till one day I was preparing the chapel in our church for a wedding. I went to light the two candles on the Communion table. There wasn't the slightest draft inside the church; in fact, it was perfectly calm outside. The matches would light and burn, but every time I tried to touch the flame to the candlewick a "wind" blew the flame away. The wind could not be felt; I could only see the flame lie right down parallel to the floor, always blowing away from the candle, and I could hear the rustle of the wind on the flame. I knew who was causing it. At first I didn't know why. Then it dawned on me. It was exactly in this way that the match did not make contact with the propane tank. Then I turned and lit the candles . . . easily.

Other times when the angels had saved me from death dated

right back to my childhood. The last time was on the highways of Alberta, and this time was the only time I recognized their intervention when it was happening.

It is not possible in this book to record all that happened in those opening days or, indeed, since. Not only is there not enough time, but much of what took place is of a deep and personal nature. I feel, at least for the present time, that it cannot be shared. I do, however, want to say something about the spirit of these angels. Their spirit in every aspect is like the spirit of Christ. In fact, it is necessary to note one of the restraints Jesus laid upon his disciples. You will recall the disciples came to Jesus and asked him how they could know who was on God's side and who was against God. They were asking Jesus how they could be absolutely sure whom they could trust and whom they could not trust. Jesus gave his disciples this rule: "Test the spirit," he said. "If it is like my spirit, it is of me; if it is not in any way like my spirit, it is not of me."

This is still the test today. I believe that in an age to come the angels of God are going to work in close conjunction with people on earth. It is not a game. It will require many things on the part of people. I was careful to make this test many times. I became convinced then, and I remain convinced today, that these angels are exactly what they presented themselves to be— angels of God, on God's side and in God's ministry. Their spirit is rich and surely in tune with the spirit of Christ.

One aspect of their spirit was their sense of humor. It was often in evidence and they used it in many ways—one such way to help me learn to control my emotions. Here is one situation that occurred early in our encounter. I had been requested to conduct a funeral service in a chapel outside of Red Deer. On the way the angels said to me, "Ed, we want you to quiet down your delivery today."

It was not good advice and today I would not act upon it. At that time the angels knew that I would follow their suggestion and this was the idea—it was a setup for a learning situation. I did quiet down my delivery and then, right in the middle of my sermon, my head was turned toward the organist and one of the angels said, "Do you want us to set it to music?"

I did not lose either my composure or stride or betray to the congregation my emotions. I not only carried on but, sensing the situation, I returned to my own style of preaching.

On the way home I was contesting with the two for their tactics, and they took control of the steering wheel of my car on a long, sweeping curve, and speeding the car around it they said, "You drive us round the bend."

Please do not think for a moment they were trifling. They were very serious in their desire to prepare me for working with them in God's service in what may well be one kind of ministry that is to become more and more prevalent in days to come.

Their barb at me on the way home was not serious. They were simply trying to see if I could be frightened off from contesting with them. We soon began working at a higher level. In the training sessions—which were carried on right in the midst of genuine service—we often "went after one another." They would often awaken me at night, sometimes for a genuine training session and sometimes for what appeared to me mere nonsense. I would say to them, "Look, you fellows, you may neither slumber nor sleep, but I have become accustomed to at least seven hours' sleep a night. Now buzz off; I'm going back to sleep."

But I wasn't going back to sleep. They sometimes kept me awake all night. They were compelling me to work long hours and under stress. There was another deep and significant factor—they were teaching me, compelling me, to learn to trust God and depend on God for all things, even strength for each day and every task as it came. And strength always came. People continued to ask, "How do you keep going? We can't understand how you can do so much and where you get the energy."

Not only the energy came; God asked a great deal from us, and He provided a great deal for us.

During the three years that Joy and I owned our trailer—a

twenty-two-foot holiday trailer—we kept it spotted at Pine Lake, a beautiful little lake about twenty miles from our home in Red Deer. We loved to spend some evenings at our trailer and at least part of our summer holidays. Pine Lake had a special significance for us. My parents had homesteaded there early in the century. I had not seen Pine Lake until Joy and I, along with our family, began to picnic there while we ministered to one of our early pastoral charges some twenty-six miles east of Red Deer. We came to love Pine Lake together. The next events in our encounter with God were to be centered around the trailer.

III

THE TRAILER

Gaetz Memorial has a large congregation and serves a high percentage of the population of the city of Red Deer and the surrounding district. Demands for ministerial service are constant. During my ministry, every week brought requests for funeral services, marriages and counseling. One afternoon while conducting a funeral service in Eventide Chapel, I noticed a new clarity and resonance in my voice. I immediately thought a sound system had been installed and I was impressed with the quality. As I continued to conduct the service, I looked around for the speakers and the controls. None were in sight, and I could not see a microphone. Again I was impressed. As the service continued, I was listening to my voice and could hear it being projected into every corner and every area of the chapel. My voice was being distributed evenly throughout the whole chapel. When the service was over, I forgot about the sound system and went on my pastoral rounds. I did not think of it again until the next funeral in the chapel. The same thing happened.

Now I was curious—where was the "mike," the speakers, the control panel? Riding to the cemetery with the funeral director I complimented him on the new sound system and asked him how he could conceal it so well. He was dumbfounded; he said, "We don't have a sound system."

"You don't! I thought you had come up with something ingenious."

This time he just looked at me as if I had lost my grip on life. I let the matter drop, the mystery still unsolved.

The phenomenon continued and not just at funerals. It began to happen during weddings. Gaetz Memorial had a most effective sound system but it was not used at weddings. The sound system that came on during weddings was even more perfect. I could hear my voice being projected into every corner and again spread evenly throughout the entire sanctuary. Now I knew it was not a sound system and I knew it was a gift from God—a beautiful gift. It gave me a great deal of pleasure, of joy. So far I had not mentioned this to anyone. Within myself I called it "my sound system voice." It continued for many weeks; then it began to "switch on" and "switch off." At no time did I have control over the coming on or the going off. It would come on in the middle of a service and go off while the service was still in progress. I had to make quick adjustments in the use of my voice. I was always delighted when my sound system voice came on, and a little bit sorry when it was turned off.

Summer holiday time came and Joy and I spent the first few days relaxing at our trailer. One beautiful summer morning we were preparing to have our breakfast on our picnic table alongside the trailer. There seemed to be no one but the two of us in sight. I turned to say something to Joy just as she stepped out of the trailer with our breakfast in her hands. My sound system voice came on in full volume. It was Joy who was surprised; she looked startled and said, "What was that?"

"Sit down, dear, and let me tell you what has been happening. It started last fall. . . ." And I told her the story.

The matter was then dropped for a while. A few moments later one of my angels said to me, "Ed, God wants you to know that when he wants you to be heard you will be heard."

I made no comment. What could I say? I have never forgotten that statement; I have pondered it in my mind ever since.

My sound system voice soon ceased to come on. It has been many months now since I last heard it.

A few days later on another glorious, sunny morning at beautiful Pine Lake, my angels said to me, "Ed, put on a clean shirt."

It was an unusual request for I had a clean shirt on; however, I took a short-sleeved shirt that Joy had just pressed, and pressed so well that the breastpocket was ironed closed. It did not matter; I was not going to put anything into the pocket, so I patted it as if to say, "O.K., stay closed."

My angels then said, "Ed, we want you to go for a walk; go to the left side of the lake and walk to the top of that hill."

They had pointed to a part of the lake that was not easy to get to and where people almost never went. The hill was not terribly high and not far away. To get to it you had to go around or go over a little inlet of water, climb through a barbed wire fence and scramble through some trees that caused you to bend over to miss the low branches.

As I came out of the trees into the clearing at the top of the hill and straightened up from my bending under the branches, I felt something enter my shirt breastpocket. I put my hand on the pocket and felt a short object, about an inch long and round like a small stick. I thought that a piece of branch had snapped off and entered my pocket. It was sufficiently uncomfortable for me to reach in and throw it away. It was not a stick, and it had not entered my pocket by accident. It was not one object, but two.

To my utter surprise—and great delight—I took out of my pocket and held in my hand an object that I had never before seen. The middle part was wrapped in a silvery substance with a sort of tinfoil look. At both ends the tips were black and dwindled down to almost a point. There was a little bit of printing on the silver part, but it did not make any recognizable sense. The second object was a small safety pin. I looked at the strange object in silence for the longest time. I had felt the objects go into my pocket. The pocket was now completely unsealed. I knew the angels had placed the two objects in my pocket. I did not know what they could possibly mean.

"You gave these to me, didn't you?" I said.

"No-o-o, they represent a gift from God."

God had already given me many gifts; high among the most precious of these was the gift of my wife, Joy, and the gifts of our children.

I continued to examine these new acquisitions carefully, particularly the strange object of silver and black with its equally strange markings. I held it in my fingers. I squeezed it; I turned it in every direction. It was very hard; apart from that, I could decipher nothing about it. Finally I asked, "What do these mean?"

"Well, they mean that God loves you; you will know more about these gifts later."

I had one more question, "Will God give Joy a gift like these in a similar manner?"

"Yes, He will," came their reply.

I hurried back to the trailer to show these strange objects to Joy and to tell her how they had come into my possession and share with her my elation at receiving such gifts in such a manner. I did one thing more; I told her that she would receive a similar gift. This proved to be both wrong and right. I place the "wrong" first, for that is the order of time. Joy did not receive an object such as I had received either at that time or later. It was to be a long time before we had knowledge of what these objects signified or understood the conversation that had taken place with the angels immediately after they had given these gifts to me.

It was, in fact, six years after the walk on the hill by beautiful Pine Lake that the interpretation was given to us. The objects were not meant to be gifts in themselves. They were symbols—symbols of gifts that God had already given to both Joy and myself, and the assurance that these gifts would be given to us both in greater proportions in years to come. The strange black object represented the uncommon, something or someone from a realm beyond the earth. It represented angels of God from the eternal realm. The safety pin represented the common, something or someone from the earth plane of life. The objects together simply stated that God had permitted his angels to work in cooperation with both Joy and myself. This had been going on from the moment of birth. These objects were presented to me at this time to let us know that God now was giving us the knowledge that for so long had been hidden from us, that we were privileged to work with His angels. The objects represented this much more—that from now on both Joy and I would work with God's angels not only conscious of the relationship, but that the scope of the work would be greatly broadened in a new ministry.

For several months I carried these objects with me, always placing them in my left breastpocket. I did not tell many people about them, only the immediate family and one or two close friends. One friend, after a long and careful examination and quiet deliberation, made this interpretation, "Ed, this means that heaven and earth are going to work together."

Finally I took the objects, wrapped them in collophane and put them in a small safety box I keep in my desk. They have remained there ever since.

The unusual continued to occur on our holidays. We took our trailer into the Canadian Rockies and stayed for a few days at Banff, Alberta. We then went into the Okanagan Valley for another week. Wherever we were in our trailer, our children (five of them: four sons and one daughter, three of them by this time married) would come to us. They shared to a large extent in all that was happening in our lives. They were most interested and all of them had some experience of their own of the presence of God through his ministry of angels.

In the Okanagan the weather is hot and stable. The valley is noted for its climate and its fruit. We languished in the sunshine and stayed cool by stretching out in our beach chairs by the lakeside. Before our stay was over, one of my angels said, "Ed, we think you should start for home."

"For home? It's beautiful here. We don't want to go home till our time is up."

"There is a storm coming, and we think you should be home before it hits."

After a pause, I said, "Can we stay one more day, two more days?"

"One more day and then you had better be on your way—and early."

We left early on the morning of the second day and decided that we would take the trailer back to Pine Lake and spend a few days there. We arrived safely and the weather was fine—for two days. Then a summer thunderstorm hit and there was hail as big as hens' eggs. The storm was bad enough at the lake, but it was much worse in town. We had received only the tail end. Trailers that were out in the storm in Red Deer looked like someone had taken a hammer and systematically pounded them over their entire surface. Many houses were severely damaged, especially the roofs. A tree on the front lawn of our home was split right in two, each side lying flat on the ground.

The storm was soon over and the sun was shining again. We settled back in our trailer to enjoy the few days of holiday still remaining. In my mind I began to ponder all that awaited me on my return to the office. My angels broke into my thoughts saying, "Ed, we don't think you are going to stand up to your first few days back at work."

Actually I felt wonderful and I was ready to go back to work. I thought my angels were pulling my leg. I said, "Quit kidding, you fellows, get serious."

"Oh, we are serious," they replied, "and you'd better get serious. You are not going to stand up to your first few days back."

Perhaps they were serious about something. I felt I had better find out what it was all about.

"O.K., O.K., what's on your mind?"

"You are going to have an operation."

"An operation!" I exclaimed. "Now you are kidding. I'm as healthy as a horse."

"Oh, you think you are, do you?"

"All right, what kind of an operation?"

"You are going to have your appendix out."

"You must be putting me on. My appendix has never bothered me."

"That isn't all. When the doctor goes in to remove your appendix, he is going to find something else."

They then described something most unusual. I feel it is of such a deep personal nature that I wish not to reveal it here. At the time I was not sure that what I had heard would come to pass; but then, I was not sure that it would not. For a time I could not dismiss the conversation, but I kept it entirely to myself. It was not the kind of thing to be discussed with anyone.

On the night before our holidays ended the angels kept me awake a great part of the time. Nevertheless, the next morning I was at my desk right on time and feeling fine. I began immediately to sort out all that had gathered on my desk during my absence. At the same time my mind was pushing ahead to the week that was before me and to the Sunday services that were coming. Thus all other thoughts were crowded out.

All of a sudden I felt a great stabbing pain across the lower part of my back. I straightened up rigidly. I winced and pressed both hands against the pain in my back.

"Oh no!" I sat still for a moment and then the pain subsided. I said, "To heck with you guys. I've got work to do," and I set to it once more. Not for long. The pain came again. It was so severe I could hardly bear it. It was still in my back and I said, "That's not an appendix pain."

But it moved around to the front and then I was sick. I looked up at my clock on the wall; it was twenty minutes to eleven. I rang for my secretary and told her that I was having difficulty and must go home. From home I called the hospital and spoke to my friend, Dr. Ronald Douglas. He said, "You'd better get into the hospital as fast as you can. Do you want me to send an ambulance?"

"No, I think I can drive my own car."

"Are you sure? There is no need to."

"I'll be all right. I'll need about half an hour."

"Come to Emergency and have the nurse let me know the minute you get there. I'll come right down."

I then phoned out to the lake and asked them to have Joy call me. It was no time at all. As we spoke on the phone, I was the sickest I had been all morning. I could hardly talk.

"Oh, honey, I'm so sick," I said.

"Darling, what is it?" Joy answered with obvious alarm in her voice.

"It's my appendix. Doug is going to take it out this afternoon." I always called my friend "Dr. Doug," or just plain "Doug."

"I'll be right in. Do you want me to come and drive you to the hospital?"

"No, dear, I'll drive over; I'll see you in Emergency."

By the time I was admitted to Emergency my temperature had dropped to slightly below normal, the pain had gone and there was no indication of any sickness. Joy, with our youngest son David, arrived before the doctor. She could see that I was feeling better. She was being, as always, most perceptive and most helpful. She said, "When the doctor comes, don't you tell him what the trouble is. Let him tell you."

Dr. Doug examined me carefully, then he said, "You haven't

any sign of appendicitis, Ed, but I think we had better keep you in and do some exploring and see what is wrong."

I was admitted to a delightful room in a new wing and put straight to bed. Joy and David left to go home for a short time and I was alone. By now I was completely furious with my angels.

"Do you mind telling me what I am doing here?"

"You need a doctor."

"A doctor! What on earth for?"

"You need a hospital too."

For the rest of the afternoon the nurses prepared me for X rays and about seven-thirty the next morning I was in the X-ray room beginning a series of exposures that were to take two and one-half hours. My system had been completely emptied. I had not had anything to eat or drink since being admitted.

After two hours of X rays at regular intervals the technician said, "Now, I want you to lie still for twenty minutes. I want one more picture. Just relax, don't move, I'll be back in twenty minutes."

I was glad to lie still and not even think. It was a rather deep stillness. I did not even blink. In twenty minutes the nurse was back saying, "I want you to go into the bathroom and make sure every bit of liquid is out of the way; then get up on the table for one final X ray."

There could be no liquid left in me; I felt sure of that. However, obediently I went into the bathroom and sat down. Instantly there was a free movement and I rose and turned to gaze on my appendix and the rest of the operation as it had been foretold to me by the angels. I had seen appendixes before. My doctor friends had shown me freshly removed ones and pointed out interesting things about them. There was no doubt in my mind. I studied the appendix, the whole situation. I took in every detail of how the cut was made. The appendix was healthy —slightly enlarged, but not discolored or marked in any way.

My own mind was certain. After many moments I flushed the toilet. It did not occur to me to call either the doctor or the nurse. I have pondered this in my mind through the years. There is a lingering doubt in my mind as to my wisdom—or lack of it. Today I definitely would have sought confirmation.

Of course, I thanked my angels. I always do. They acknowledge my thanks, but from time to time they say to me, "Thank God, not us."

I always do that also. I thank him over and over for blessings, for His wondrous love, for His amazing presence, for miracles, for strength for each day, for His grace, for all things so lavishly given.

Does an encounter with two of God's angels in a matter so personal, so delicate, so private as this have any place in a book such as this one I write to present to any who will read it? I believe it does.

First of all, like all the events described in this book, it actually happened and happened exactly as I have recorded it. A further significance is this—here was one more time the angels had intervened to save my life. One question that arises is, "Could the doctors, many of whom are my friends, not have performed this operation?" Well, of course, they could. It is my opinion, however, that the doctors would not have had any opportunity to detect the malfunction in my body until it had reached a stage so far advanced that it would be too late to save me from a life at least less than one of good health. I believe the angels foresaw something that might have been, and intervened to spare me from a long drawn-out illness and an operation that would likely have left me less than a whole person.

In my mind there is at least one more significance and one perhaps of greater importance. I believe that in many cases, not in every case, but in many, where doctors treat patients and perform operations, the angels of God lend assistance to effect cures. The ministering of angels in most of these cases goes entirely undetected by both the doctor and the patient. One of my doctor friends who is a gifted surgeon often shares with me situations he encounters in practicing medicine and performing surgery. He told me of one particular operation where the patient was an elderly lady. Before he had completely finished the surgical procedure the anesthetist said to him that he could no longer keep the patient safely under the anesthetic. The surgeon decided that the risk of continuing the operation was greater than the risk of terminating it and acted accordingly. As he described the operation to me it was evident he had given the matter a great deal of thought. He concluded the description with these words, "The patient really should not have made a complete recovery, but she did."

He was very thoughtful about the whole thing. He also told me that the doctors who assisted in the operation chided him, "You're just plain lucky."

I listened with great interest, and, like my doctor friend, this story lingered in my mind through the years. At the time I had no answers to offer. Today I am convinced that here was one time when the angels of God assisted a doctor in bringing a surgical procedure to a successful conclusion. In so doing the angels undoubtedly prolonged the life on earth of a human being. For a few days Dr. Doug wished to keep me in the hospital. During this time the angels of God gave me the option to withdraw from this new encounter. This was not the first time they had given me this opportunity. I chose to continue. It was not quite that simple but that was the gist of it. My decision to go on in this thrilling encounter has never wavered. Let me say again—it is not a game. It is a demanding relationship and calls for thorough preparation, constant vigilance, daily prayer, complete trust in God, and many, many, many sacrifices. My decision to go on in this ministry with two of God's angels led to the next "surprise."

The day of the X ray was Wednesday. The following Saturday I was scheduled to perform three weddings. One was for the daughter of one of the doctors in the congregation. He visited me every day and said, "Ed, you have got to be out of here by Friday."

"Tell that to Doug," was my reply. "He is the only one keeping me here."

Doug released me from the hospital after lunch on Friday. That evening I conducted three wedding rehearsals. On Saturday I performed the wedding ceremonies and attended two of the receptions. On Sunday I conducted the services of worship.

IV

BATHED BY
INVISIBLE HANDS

About halfway through the first week after my return home from the hospital, I rose early one morning and entered the bathroom to prepare for another day. One of my angels said, "Ed, fill the bathtub with water."

I did so, and they told me to get in the tub. I did. Then invisible hands took the soap and the facecloth and washed me all over. There was the clear unmistakable touch of four hands washing my body all over. The feel of the hands was quite clear and distinct. There was a firmness to the pressure. The lather was very real. They poked their fingers into my ears and into every private area of my body. They rinsed off the soap, told me to step out of the tub, took a towel and dried me. Then one of them said, "From this moment on we are going to have our hands in every area of your life."

I made no reply, but I have often pondered this moment, and, believe me, their hands have indeed been in every aspect of my life constantly ever since.

Not many days later one of the angels said to me, "Ed, do you trust God?"

"You know I do," I answered.

"But, Ed, we want to know—do you really trust God?"

"You know that I do."

"All right, Ed, God wants to know if you will trust him by placing your wife completely in His hands?"

"Yes." My mind was racing ahead. Did I have the right to commit Joy to something I did not fully understand? On the other hand, I had always committed my wife, my family, my friends, my own life completely into the hands of God. But was the surrender to God full and complete, or did I say I was placing my loved ones in His hands and then act as if I was in full control? Finally I realized that there is nothing better you can do with your life, your wife, your husband—all those you love or all your aspirations—than to place them fully in the hands of God.

"Yes, I will entrust my wife completely to God."

"You realize that this means you will not interfere with God's decisions for her, you will really let go?"

"I understand that."

The bargain was struck. It was to prove a most difficult assignment, and there was to be a great deal of pain. The next morning in the chapel at our church, as humbly as I could, I committed Joy once more into the hands of God.

The demands on my time increased: a constant line of people came to my office to seek help with a variety of needs. Training with the angels went on night and day. True to their word, they were into every area of my life and ministry. With their help wonderful things happened in the lives of many who came to my office, some of them strangers to me and some from many miles away. It was a source of amazement, satisfaction and joy.

Toward the end of January, in the dead of winter, Joy came to me one evening and said, "I think I would like to go to Vancouver and spend some time with Margaret."

Margaret was our only daughter and number three in the family. She had married a young university student who had graduated from the University of Alberta and was now attending Simon Fraser University in Vancouver studying for his master's degree in science. They had an infant son, Paul.

"I think I should tell you," Joy continued, "that I may not come back."

"Hands off, Ed," that was the bargain. My mind was working. "One has to remember," I told myself, "that God gave us a mind and he expects us to use our intelligence at all times and in all circumstances." The last thing I wanted was for Joy to leave me. Joy went on speaking, "It's not that I don't love you, but I need time to think. Anyway, I'll write to you."

"All right, honey. Can I make reservations for you? If you will let me know when you want to go, I'll make the arrangements. I just want to say that I love you more than words can tell, and I hope you will come back."

Joy went to Vancouver. She stayed one month. During that time we not only wrote to each other, we also spoke on the telephone many times. I tried to be as loving as I could in every outreach I made to her. When she returned our relationship was stronger than before, but it had not seen its last test nor its last trial. Let me say again, it is not possible to put into words what Joy and I have gone through. I am sure that it has been even more difficult for Joy. Through it all we have continued to grow in strength and in many other ways. We continue to grow in understanding of each other and in our total relationship. I would be amiss if I did not praise Joy for her loyalty to me and her devotion to God. Entrusting Joy's life to God, completely to God, in this new circumstance was in many ways beautiful; it was, however, far, far from easy.

Surprises continued to come almost without ceasing. One

evening I rose up from my favorite chair and began walking down the hallway of our home toward our bedroom. As I entered the hall the weight lifted from my body and I "rose up," and for three steps I skimmed over the floor not touching it. Then my body was "put down" and I continued to walk on my own feet, not missing a stride. In a flash the only thought in my mind was this; "That is how Jesus walked on water; his body was lifted by God's ministering angels."

Many times since, the weight has been partly lifted from my body and I walk lightly; however, I was only that once lifted completely from the floor.

In the fall of one of the early years—1972—quite a different phenomenon began to happen. Just after I had pronounced the Benediction at the end of a morning service of worship, a stabbing pain came very high up on the inside of my right groin. I winced. For a brief instant I froze. It was soon gone. This became a standard practice at the conclusion of every Sunday morning service. The pain was very sharp and increased in intensity. Then it began to occur during the Benediction and then just as I was starting the Benediction. It was both painful and irritating and it puzzled me greatly. I was convinced then, and I remain convinced to this day, that the pain was an infliction placed upon me by my angels. Just why I do not know.

After many weeks the pain began to occur on other days. It continued to occur often and with greater intensity. Finally it became a daily occurrence and sometimes lasted the whole day through. There were times when I was given a whole day without the pain. Such days were glorious.

In the end, the stabbing pain caused a hernia to appear. At first it was small, but it grew until it was very large. Like the pain, at times the hernia was taken completely away and I would be totally healed. Then it would return. For many months no one but myself knew about the hernia. Twice I had gone to Dr. Doug for examination, but the hernia was completely healed and he did not detect it. For about eighteen months this hernia was used by the angels as a source of torment and irritation to my flesh. They would send a sort of wave through the hernia causing the liquid to bubble. It was one of the worst torments I have ever known and caused me to work under great pressure. This was likely part of the purpose but I do not think it was the whole reason.

In my own mind I felt sure that this hernia had been given to me by my angels and thus with the consent of God. I felt equally sure that God would heal the hernia. My course of action was to await this day. It was not only a long time coming, it did not come in a manner that I had expected. I felt sure, too, that the hernia would remain my secret. It was not to be.

One day as I lay on the examination table in Dr. Doug's office, the hernia began to appear. It was only slightly revealed but Doug saw it.

"What have you been lifting? he asked.

I had not been lifting anything.

"The only thing we can do with a hernia is cut it out. If it gets any bigger I think you should have an operation."

An operation was not in my plans. I was sure God would heal it. In the last few years he had healed other parts of my body. Let me share two of these healings with you.

Our family had taken a holiday by train from Ottawa, where we were ministering in Bell Street United Church, to Edmonton, where we had once lived and where some of my brothers and sisters still lived. On a dark, rainy evening I stepped off the train as it stopped at a small station just outside of Winnipeg. I thought the trainman had placed the stool at the foot of the steps. He had not and I took a real tumble. The side of my heel caught on the side of a stone, and I hit with the whole force of my body and twisted the ankle, badly tearing the ligaments. The ankle swelled to the size of a large orange and the pain was tremendous. So were my screams. For several years after I had a weak and often painful ankle. One summer day at the trailer I asked God if He would heal it, and He did instantly. It has been well and strong ever since.

There was another interesting healing. I was delivering a tall, narrow package to one of the board members of our church. The package was like a man's suit box. I could hold the parcel from one end with my hands. It was in the mid evening and I did what I had become accustomed to doing—I rang the doorbell and then opened the door and started to walk in. I was not aware that my friends had a large dog who was rather protective of the home. As I stepped through the door, he came galloping down the hall at full speed, and his intentions were clearly evident in his eyes and face. I attempted to thrust the parcel between myself and the dog. He took one leap in my direction and got hold of my exposed hand. He bit right through the nail of my right index finger and got a fair chunk of my thumb also. My hand bled profusely. By now my host had come on the scene and separated the dog and me and looked at my hand. He was most distressed and bathed it in cold water and bandaged it as best he could. I got into my car, and as I started to drive home I said a simple prayer asking God to heal my hand. The throbbing pain left immediately, and by the next day there was not a mark on my hand—it was healed completely and permanently.

This incident occurred on a Thursday night. In church the next Sunday my friend hurried over to me to inquire about my hand. Concern was etched on his face as he greeted me with these words, "How is your hand?"

"It's fine," I answered, "God healed it."

The expression on his face changed to surprise and perhaps one of a little skepticism.

"Do you mind if I see it?" he asked rather timidly.

I stretched out to him my right hand without a mark or a blemish on it. He took it in his hand and turned it in every direction, examining it carefully. Then his face lit up in a smile. He was convinced of the healing and pleased to see it.

Thus I was sure that God would heal the hernia. Of course, He did—but not in the manner that I expected. He made me go through the operation. That was, however, not to happen for several months. Other things had to happen first.

One of the "other things" that was to happen was that Joy was to discover the hernia. It had come up very large one evening, and Joy brushed against it and said, "What on earth is that?"

"It's a hernia, dear," I replied as casually as I could.

"How did you ever get a thing like that?"

Still striving to be casual, I replied, "My angels gave it to me."

Joy did not answer in words. Her facial expression spoke volumes. She was not prepared to believe what I had said.

Finally she said, "That is like saying God gave it to you."

"Yes, in a way."

"Well, I won't believe that. Don't ask me to believe that."

I was no longer casual. I replied, "But I am asking you to believe that because it is true. The angels"—suddenly they were not "my angels"—"gave me this hernia over a period of several months in as systematic a way as you could ever imagine."

"Well, I won't believe it," Joy replied with great feeling. "Just don't ask me to believe that a loving Father would treat one of His faithful ministers like that."

Joy could not be convinced—not by me. This was one of the lessons I had to learn. I had to learn also that when God wishes someone to believe, He will cause it to happen. This was just one more thing I had to learn to leave in the hands of God.

Joy's reasoning was right. But did it go far enough? It is a question I too had to struggle with. It was difficult for me to understand why a loving Father would inflict this kind of torment. In my reasoning my mind turned to Jesus. After all, a loving Father asked Jesus to endure the cross. We have learned to speak so easily about the Crucifixion. So often we seem to lose sight of the tremendous pain, the great injustice, the incredible humiliation, to say nothing of the struggle that Jesus went through to know for sure whether or not his father, his loving Father, was really asking him to die on a cross.

I did not say any of this to Joy; we did not speak of the

matter any further at that point. Other thoughts entered my mind. I wondered at the time and have wondered since, whether it was possible that God was preparing me to face rejection. I did not know then and I still do not know for sure. There has been rejection. It has not surprised me. In fact, I have been more surprised by the great numbers of people who have had firsthand experience with God's ministering angels. When I ask them why they have not told others of their experience they say, "I was afraid that people would not believe me," or, "I thought people might think I was foolish."

This was not to be the only torment to my flesh, my mind and my soul that I was to experience. I cannot pretend to understand all the reasons why. I do believe that God calls men and women into his service, and I am convinced that God uses His own ways to prepare them for tasks He is going to entrust to their hands.

One thing seems certain: when you say, "I walk and talk with God's angels," you have come close enough to God to experience at firsthand the mystery of the ways in which he moves, "His wonders to perform."

V

A SPECIAL KIND
OF COUNSELING

The great joys and the abundant blessings of these days far outweighed the burdens. One of the great joys came from a special kind of counseling that developed without any conscious move on my part. Counseling had always held an important place in my ministry. People of all ages came to me with their problems and they often sent their friends. Now a new dimension was added.

First, let me share something with you as part of the background. At one point, when my angels were discussing some aspects of my ministry, one of them said, "Ed, you do not seem to be aware of it, but your ministry is a ministry of love. God has given you a great gift of love for people. Wherever you go your love is a healing force; when you leave a pastoral charge you leave behind a great group of people who love you."

I had not known that. I did recognize that I had a genuine

49

love for people. It was so natural that I had never had to give
any special thought to it. It was just there; it had always been
there. Then the angel said, "From your birth God has surrounded
you with loving people; your parents were loving people; your
sister, Winnie, poured out a reckless love on you when you were
small—you were 'her baby.' And one reason God gave you
Joy for your wife is that she not only is a very loving person,
but your love for her deepens your ability to minister."

People had always come to me for counseling: they often
said, "You are so easy to talk to."

Now I recognized that people were coming with new kinds
of problems, and some of them came from long distances. Let me
share with you just two special cases. The first is a young married
couple from within the congregation.

After church one Sunday morning a young wife and mother
of two small children stayed behind to speak with me and ask
for a counseling appointment. She said that she and her husband
had a problem that was destroying their marriage, and unless
something was done about it they might actually break up. I
assumed that it was a normal marriage problem but made no
comment. An appointment was made for early in the week ahead.
On the hour of the appointment it was her husband who came
and he was alone. I was surprised but let the interview unfold
without comment. Soon he was talking freely saying, "I have a
dream; I have it nearly every night. It frightens me, and I wake up
and usually my wife wakes up too. We don't know how to handle
the situation."

"Tell me your dream."

"Well, I have an uncle; he died a few months ago and I had
to make all the funeral arrangements. He had bought a grave in a
cemetery in a little village about sixty miles from here. I'm not
even sure I found the right grave. My uncle was a bachelor and
had always lived alone. We were the only relatives he had."

I will call this man Mr. T. He went on, "In this dream I am
standing beside the grave, and he is lying there in the open coffin.

I am looking down at him. Then all of a sudden we change places; I am lying in the coffin and my uncle is standing over me looking down at me and smiling. That's when I wake up. It's driving us both crazy and we are getting so tired."

I listened intently; at the same time I was silently asking God in a prayer to please reveal to me the meaning of this dream and help me to help this young man and his wife. Then I asked Mr. T. to tell me all he could about the funeral and to tell me the dream again. The only new thing that Mr. T. added was that both he and his wife were concerned about the eternal destiny of their uncle's soul.

"We don't think he ever went to church—we just don't know."

I was awaiting some help from my angels. They often made me use all my knowledge before they stepped in. Finally one of them said, "Tell Mr. T. that this dream does not mean that someone else in his family is going to die."

It had been obvious that Mr. T. thought this might be an announcement of his own death. I gave him that message and he was greatly relieved.

The next message that was spoken into my ear did not seem so comforting; my angel said, "Tell Mr. T. his uncle says, 'You are more dead than I am.' "

"Would you mind saying that again?"

"Certainly, tell Mr. T. that his uncle says, 'You are more dead than I am.' "

To Mr. T. I said, "I think I am beginning to understand your dream. I think your uncle is trying to tell you that actually you are more dead than he is."

The surprise showed clearly on Mr. T.'s face.

"Here, I'll type that out for you," I went on, and I did.

Then the message began to clear up. I said to Mr. T., "The only real life there is, is the life we shall inherit in God's eternal kingdom. Your uncle is alive for the first time. He is so gloriously alive that by comparison you, Mr. T., are not alive at all.

Your uncle smiles at you in the dream because he is amused at the little things you worry about and let spoil your life and your marriage. Everything you did for him was good. All is well. All is well with your uncle. You are worrying for no reason. Would you like me to type that out for you also?"

As Mr. T. read the typed copy over a few times, he began to smile. He had no difficulty seeing and believing it all. We talked for a while longer; then as he began to leave, I said, "You will not have that dream again." And he didn't. Their marriage returned to normal and their gratitude was evident in the warmth of their greeting each Sunday.

The second case in this special kind of counseling that I wish to share with you was with a man who was not a member of the congregation and whom I had not seen or heard of before. He just suddenly showed up at my office one day right after lunch, and my secretary let him in before I had returned. She said, "He needed to see you so badly."

I protested mildly but conceded, and out of the corner of my eye I could see my secretary smiling as I opened the door to go into my office as if to say, "I knew you would see him."

The man was in his mid to late thirties, married, and he and his wife had a boy and a girl about ten and twelve. He was very tense but began to talk immediately. He said, "I have a dream almost every night. It is spoiling our marriage. I have been to a doctor and he sent me to a psychologist, but I am still having the dream."

"Would you tell me the dream?"

He sat on the edge of the chair and said, "In this dream I am taking a picture of my wife and the children. She is in the middle and she has one arm around each of the children. I take the picture but when I have it developed everything is black. You can just see the outline of my wife and the children. I'm afraid . . ."

I finished the sentence for him, "You're afraid someone in the family is going to die?"

"Yes, or maybe something awful is going to happen to all three of them."

As I listened I had been asking God in prayer for help in interpreting the dream and assisting this young man.

"No, the dream does not indicate anyone is going to die or be physically hurt." That much I had been told, but no more.

Sometimes I could be a little impatient with the angels; they took their own time. This was one such occasion. I did not know the interpretation and I was not being told.

"Tell me the dream again, please, and try to put every little detail in."

There was not the slightest change in what he had said before. Nor was there any help from the angels. At moments like this they were just "angels," not "my angels."

"Did anything happen in your life or in your family just before you began to have this dream?"

At first the man said, "No." After a little drawing out he told me an incident that was very painful for him to talk about. He said, "Last fall my father and I went on a big game hunting trip. While we were on the trip my father got a heart attack. I was afraid to try to move him. I left him and went for help, but when I got back he was dead. I shouldn't have left him."

The young man was hitting the chair with his fist and at the point of breakdown. Now the angels began to speak to me.

"Tell the young man he could not have prevented his father's death. Tell him that his father is alive and well in God's kingdom and that he has nothing to worry about."

I told him these things.

"Tell him also that he is killing the family love that exists between his wife and children and himself. That is what the black in the picture signifies."

I gave him this message. There was a little more in the message, and I passed all of it along to him. We talked for a while longer. He was relaxing and obviously beginning to function with a new freedom.

It became apparent now why the angels held back their message so long. The young man had a great deal to get off his chest. He had to learn to speak about his father's death; he had to get rid of his feelings of guilt.

Before he left we prayed together. As he went through the door, I told him he would not have this dream again. He never did. The family love returned and blossomed.

People continued to come from the congregation, from the city, from the surrounding area, from other churches, and from many miles away. Not all had special problems. Some came with the ordinary problems of life that all of us face. Many were helped; many were healed. The love of God flowed in the most beautiful way through the ministry of his angels, and it flowed even through my ministry.

Not all were helped and not all were healed.

One day a young minister and his wife from a long distance away came to my study. The minister had asthma and he had it bad. I was pleased that they had come. I wanted very much to be part of a healing force for this man. He was skeptical about my ability to heal. He said, "If you can heal people, why haven't you healed your wife?"

It was a fair question and a difficult one. Joy also had asthma and I had tried to heal her. I had laid my hands upon her and prayed for her healing. There seemed to be no answer. I have always believed that God would heal Joy. The minister knew of Joy's asthma and he knew that Joy was not healed. Actually God had healed Joy of other afflictions, and He had strengthened her in beautiful ways. In answer to this thrust I said, "You are right when you question my power to heal. It is not I who heals; it is God. It is not I who chooses who will be healed and who will not. This too is God's prerogative. He chooses. You are also right about Joy. I have not been able to heal her. I do not know why. I believe there is a reason but I don't know what it is.

"There are other things that must be said," I continued. "Some people have been healed when I have laid my hand upon them and asked God to heal them. When the answer is 'no' or 'not yet'—you see, sometimes the answer is 'not yet'—it is not our right to question. God's time is not always our time."

They were not saying a word. I continued, "I am learning many things these days. I am learning that we must run the risk of looking bad. By that I mean we know that everyone is not going to be healed. This must not stop us from trying again and again."

I leaned toward the minister and looking straight at him I said, "We do not know whether God will heal you or not, but I hope you will both be willing to join with me in asking God to take away your asthma."

They were both willing, in fact, eager. We joined hands and prayed together. The asthma was not healed. To my knowledge it remains unhealed to this day.

Good health is a rich blessing, but it is not the goal of life. Many a human being has served God with an infectious cheerfulness while carrying a heavy burden of broken health. Among these have been the ordained and the unordained.

At the same time as this special kind of counseling was going on, other unusual things were happening, all parallel in time. In the next chapter we will turn in yet another direction to something else that was new and different.

VI

VISIONS OF
THINGS TO COME

The summer of 1972 was coming to an end. It was early September. That September the Russian National Hockey Team was coming to Canada to play for the first time against a team of pros, an all-star team from the National Hockey League. I have always been an ardent sportsman and was greatly interested in this series. Four games were to be played in Canada and then four in Russia. Like many Canadians I had suffered great pangs of frustration at the Canadian amateur hockey teams going down in defeat at the hands of the Russian team in world competition. Like most Canadians I was certain the Canadian pros would handle the Russian players without too much difficulty—at least in Canada.

One day one of my angels said to me, "You know, Ed, the Russians are going to beat the National League team."

My reply was instant and with some indignation, "Oh no they're not."

"I think you will see they will."

And they did. The Russian team won the first game seven to three. The next morning in my office I said to my angels, "Who will win the second game?"

"No one," they answered with a grin, and after a pause they said, "it will be a tie."

"What will the score be?"

"Four all."

And it was.

Now I felt sure the Canadians would win the next two games and I said so, to which I got this reply, "Mmm, mmm, mmm, we will see."

The Canadians did win the third game, and as I sat and watched it on television, just before a Canadian goal was scored, I would feel a sharp thump on my right hip, then I would feel a sharp thump on my left hip, and about a minute later the Russian team would score.

The fourth game and the last in Canada was scheduled for Vancouver. There was no thought in my mind as to who would win—Canada, I was sure, would win. So all I asked my angels was, "What will the score be?"

They answered, "Five to two."

"Five to two," I repeated.

"No, five to three."

Up to this point I had not shared any of this information with anyone. On the afternoon of the game my good friend Bob Millar, who was at the time the chairman of the board at Gaetz Memorial, said to me, "Who is going to win the game tonight?"

"Canada," I replied, "and the score is going to be either five to two or five to three."

The score was five to three, but Russia won.

This was not the first time that I had received foreknowledge from my angels, and later that fall I was to receive from them a whole series of revelations about myself and Joy and our future. These revelations came in a form to which I had now become accustomed; however, some of them came in symbols. The symbols were clear and should have been simple to interpret. However, they were purposely tricky and I took too much for granted and thus made some mistakes that were to prove painful to me but at the same time would sharpen my perception regarding all subsequent revelations. This, of course, was partly the purpose. There was a deeper purpose, however; it was this: what was to occur to myself and also to Joy was to be very different and far more difficult than we could ever have dreamed. God was permitting us to see that all that was to happen would be within His will for us.

While my misinterpretation was to cause anguish—particularly to myself—it did not in any way change the outcome of what God knew was to happen and did not stop, or what God himself caused to happen. As events have unfolded, the meaning of many of these revelations has become clear; not all of them have yet been completely fulfilled. These revelations were not all made at one time; they came to me over a period of about one and one-half years.

There was a prelude to these revelations. It was this: well over a year before this particular series of revelations began my guiding angels said to me, "Ed, you are going to be asked to leave Gaetz Memorial United Church."

"Oh, I don't think so," I answered.

When we had departed from previous pastoral charges a great deal of sorrow had always been shown. There were, of course, always those who were glad to see us go. We were told by leading lay people in the congregations that these were in a great minority.

The subject was dropped and no more said about it in the next two years. I did, however, ponder it in my mind and wonder. I was not sure it would really happen, nor was I certain it would not.

With this background let me now share with you several of the revelations that were presented to me by my angels.

In my first vision I found myself in a World War II setting. I had been a pilot with the Royal Canadian Air Force on duty overseas. In these revelations I actually saw myself; it was kind of like watching myself in a movie or on television. Often there was no sound. Communication was either by familiar signs or by one of the angels adding some verbal comment or giving an actual interpretation. One of the great difficulties with revelations such as these is this: the event or events portrayed are lifted out of context; that is, the vision is not set in a time frame, such as we are accustomed to living by, and it is not associated with other events that will happen. Therefore, unless the angels tell you when the event will occur, you can have no certainty of the time and, most likely, of the place. In the revelations that I am going to share with you now, I was not told "why" these things would happen.

In the first revelation, the World War II setting, I saw myself standing alone. It was late in the day for it was dark. I sensed the "enemy" was near. My angels said to me, "Ed, God is going to put you in solitary confinement for a while."

Two guards started to move toward me. I could also see the confinement area—a very low building with small cells. I was not going to accept it without a struggle. I turned and ran. I wanted Joy to come with me and I knew she was near. I had some difficulty finding her, and when I did she seemed secure and could not see any reason to run away. I held my hand out to her and she took it, and we started to run toward an exit. It was uphill all the way and just when we seemed to be reaching freedom an enemy truck filled with armed soldiers came through the gate and cut off our retreat. I was taken by two guards. I was separated from Joy and the guards placed me in a room by myself.

To a certain extent the meaning was clear. At some time in the future I was going to be put in some kind of solitary confinement. I was to be separated in some way from Joy. I would not like it and would not accept it readily.

It began to happen in January of 1974. It did not all happen at once. It reached an intense pitch in September 1975. I have not totally been released at the date of this writing. Work with the angels at times has continued. Life has gone on. The confinement has been very real and I have not been able to share it with anyone. It is indescribable. I have been very much aware of God's presence. There have been moments when I have felt very much alone annd very much in the hands of "an enemy," even if the role of the enemy has been played by those who are on God's side. I believe this has been the case.

The full reason for this experience I do not know. It has certainly been a strengthening situation; that is, you find yourself gaining a strength which you feel could not likely come in any other way.

A second revelation came very shortly after receiving the one above. It was simple and direct. There was no room for misinterpretation. Except, I could not believe it would happen. It did, and how!

In this revelation I was shown a huge football, the oblong kind used in Rugby football. The football was a body with a head coming out the top, feet coming out the bottom and arms coming out each side. As it came into focus, it was clearly me in the football. As I looked at this wondrous sight, one of the angels said, "Ed, we are going to kick you all over the face of the earth."

And believe me, they have. The kicking around has been actually physical. It has also been mental. There have been physical irritations to my body that have gone on for hours on end. To say "they drive you crazy" is an understatement. That is their purpose—to make you function creatively in the midst of perpetual torment. Mostly it is both beyond describing and beyond believing. I know, for among those who have found it impossible to believe have been my own family. This is one part of the isolation I was put in. I have had to bear these pains and torments without being able to share them with anyone. And they have gone on almost constantly.

There was a gap of several weeks before the next revelation came. Before I attempt to describe it I wish to prefix it with this summary. I had been shown, by now, by the angels that God had a ministry for me to perform. It would be something more than a standard ministry. Through my ministry many people would be brought to know God and Jesus Christ. In time I would continue my ministry beyond Canada.

When the next revelation came it was in symbols. I was shown that God, through His Holy Spirit, would bring down many churches. Some would be humiliated. Some would be wounded. Some would look like they had died. Many would grow strong again. It is important for me to say that no interpretation was given to me for this revelation. It was simply left with me. Time is interpreting some of it. Some of it has not yet happened.

As the revelation continued I was shown that I would seek to move in a certain direction but would be drawn back. This could have referred to time. I was then shown that the associate minister at Gaetz Memorial would make a move before I did and his move would happen quickly and easily. This part of the revelation was soon fulfilled. The associate minister moved with no effort very suddenly to a church in Calgary, Alberta, in the spring of 1973. I was then shown that there would be a new church for me, but before I would be moved to this new church, there would be a length of time or a series of events that I would find very puzzling and also difficult to accept. This has come true. These events will be described as they happened in later chapters.

Three more revelations are relevant to this part of my life, and I wish to share them with you too. In the first, I could see two churches. I saw myself looking from some distance back at one of the churches. It was very beautiful and appeared to be wealthy. I looked at it with concern and with longing. Suddenly a friend of mine drew alongside of me from behind; that is, I had not noticed this friend coming. There were no words spoken but words were indicated. The friend stretched forth a hand toward this church. I intercepted, indicating that the church was prickly and the prickles might sting the friend's hand and might be poisonous. The friend withdrew and moved away silently. I was surprised by the person who came to my aid. One characteristic that stuck in my mind and turned out to be significant is this: this friend had two first names and used both together, as in Billy Joe.

The interpretation of this revelation was soon to come. I will share it with you in a chapter soon to follow.

The second revelation was quite short. I saw myself from behind, searching for a new church. I kept coming close to a new church, but always at the last minute the church would slip away. Suddenly Joy came running to my side. It was clear that she had come to my aid. Then the revelation ended.

In the interval of time that I have been without a church, twenty months now, Joy has come to my aid in many ways. And I do not think we have seen the full unfolding of this revelation.

The last revelation I will include here is one which to me is very important. It began with the phone ringing in our home in Red Deer and with my going over and answering. A male voice on the other end said, "This is Dr. Barclay speaking. I hear you are going to Vancouver. I will meet you there; I intend to be in Vancouver."

In this revelation the words were actually spoken. I turned from the phone and called to Joy in great excitement saying, "Honey, this is it." I had been expecting to be moved.

The voice at the other end of the telephone kept on talking, but the tone diminished and the words became indistinguishable. I could not hear one thing that could be understood. Again, I turned to Joy and said, "I can't understand a single word that he is saying."

The voice continued to become fainter and fainter. Then there was a complete silence. In a moment there was a CBC

(Canadian Broadcasting Corporation) time signal given. If you are not familiar with the time signals, they go something like this: there is a series of dots, then a voice says, "At the long dash, following the silence, the time will be . . ."

The time signal was quite distinct. It puzzled me. I have been through the period of confusion, a time, a long time when I could not understand what was happening. I have been through the period of silence. "The time" does not appear to have quite come yet. There are indications that "the time" for a new beginning is near.

Shortly after the CBC time signal, the voice came on the telephone again saying, "You are going to be moved in the fall. Your stars are very high."

The interpretation I put on this revelation was that we would be moved to Vancouver to a new church in the fall. I was partly wrong. We did move to Vancouver, but not to a church. We did move again two falls later, but not to a church.

If I had dealt with the revelation exactly as it was given, not adding a single word or thought, I might have come closer to the right interpretation. I have learned to deal with revelations and foreknowledge in a very scientific way, adding nothing, deleting nothing and verifying everything with as much information as one can gather.

I made the mistake also of putting two revelations together. I had been shown that I would be moved to a new church. That has not as yet happened. I believe it will. It may or may not be in Vancouver. That remains to be seen.

The truth is this. These revelations were not given to us so that we could know what was going to happen to us. They were given with just enough information in them that we could verify that the things that did happen were known beforehand to God and to his angels. They were given so that we would know that all that was going to happen to us God was going to permit to happen, and therefore there could be no reason to be afraid. God would let it all happen, but he would be in complete control of our lives and of events at all times. This is what we were supposed to learn from the revelations—this, and how to interpret a revelation correctly, although the only safe way is when the angels of God give the interpretation to you. Someday they will give me the whole interpretation of these revelations.

These were not the only revelations given to me. These are the ones I feel are relevant to my story at this point.

VII

STORM CLOUDS

On a cold Sunday in late February in 1973, Joy's asthma was bothering her. It always did in the sub-zero temperatures of a Canadian prairie winter. This morning Joy was physically drained from the struggle to breath and from weeks of hard work. I said to her, "You simply must stay in bed this morning and get some rest."

On mornings like this, when Joy did not accompany me to church, her first question on my return home would be, "How was the service this morning?"

This Sunday her question was different. She asked, "How was the congregation this morning?"

I was elated from the morning. I replied, "Honey, the only way I can describe it is to say they were a loving congregation."

"I know what you mean," Joy said. "They have been like that for quite a while. You actually feel the spirit of love that has grown among us."

We were not the only ones to comment on the rich, happy spirit that prevailed not only during the service but throughout the week.

Like most churches throughout the whole world, Gaetz Memorial had gone through the years of the declining congregation. The movement of people in the western world was part of the new phenomenon of life. Not only did people move often but when they moved even staunch church people would take time out from their association with the church. The most often repeated phrase of the newcomer to any city was, "We have decided to take a year or two out from the church."

Many did not return.

By the seventies, in Red Deer as elsewhere, the church had leveled out and once again was on the upswing. Included in the upswing, many of us felt, was a genuine deepening of our spiritual life and the quality of our worship.

Nor were Joy and our friends the only ones who felt this way. People from other churches in Red Deer and the surrounding area began to attend our services of worship from time to time. I noticed a young couple, strangers to me, attending our service in the morning, and I thought perhaps they were newcomers in town. I asked them if they would like to join our church. This was their answer, and there was a radiant congeniality about them as we talked, "We are members of another church here in Red Deer. We don't feel we should leave our own church, but something happens during worship here; there is a definite presence; we feel it every time we come. We just have to come once in a while."

During the second week of March of that year, about three weeks after Joy and I had been so uplifted by the loving spirit of our congregation, a man, a member of the congregation, came into my office. I will call this man Mr. X. It was a weekday morning. I asked if I could take his coat; he declined. I offered him a seat; again he declined. He remained standing and brought up one or two rather insignificant matters and then turned and moved toward the door. He opened the door, paused, then quickly closed the door and came back into the center of the room. He stood facing me squarely and said, "There are a few of us who think it is time you left Gaetz Memorial Church."

I made no reply. He went on, and his voice softened, "You have done a real good job, but some of us feel it is time for a change."

"I want to thank you for coming and telling me this, Mr. X. I'm sure it has taken a great deal of courage to say what you have. Do you mind telling me who the other people are that feel this way?"

"No, I'm not going to say. But they are all your friends."

He turned now and moved toward the door and opened it again. Then once more he turned and took a step back into the room and said, "And if you don't go, we are going to get together and make sure you do."

To this I made no reply, and he was gone.

I sat quietly for a few moments and pondered what I had heard. I weighed it in the light of my own assessment of what the great bulk of the congregation felt and what was best for the church. This man's antagonism against me was well known, not only to me but to others in the congregation who had spoken to me about it. I decided that I would not mention this encounter to anyone—not anyone—not my wife, my family or the church board. My decision was made on many grounds: First, this had not come from any board or committee in the church; it was a private opinion. Second, I felt my orders must come from God, and there had been no concrete indication that the time for me to move had come, and yet, there lingered in my mind, "Ed, you are going to be asked to leave Gaetz Memorial United Church."

Was this to what they had referred? I actually hoped so. This was purely one man's opinion. There were ways he could process his opinion through the boards of the congregation.

For a fleeting moment I hoped that this might be to what the angels referred concerning my being asked to leave, yet I felt it was not. I felt and rather feared that something more was yet to come.

March passed, summer came, and with it one event that had been foretold—our associate minister received a call to a church in Calgary. It came as quickly and was processed as easily as the revelation had indicated it would. The call was effective the first of August of that year.

Joy and I took our holidays in July. We spent them in "Beautiful British Columbia." We stayed with our daughter, Margaret, and her husband, Doug, for a few days in Vancouver and then on to Victoria to bask in the peace and beauty by the sea in this wonderful island paradise. The holiday was just what we needed. We left our cares and our burdens behind and enjoyed having each other all to ourselves. By this time, our children who were not married were far too mature to holiday with mom and dad. In August we returned home to our church and our work.

The fall of 1973 was to bring us to a turning point and into a new series of events in our encounter with God through his angels, and in our ministry, and in our lives. Before we look at the fall of 1973 and these events, there are two more important aspects in my life and ministry that I wish to share with you. The second of these I call "the Group"; the first and foremost of these is someone who is my surest source of help and encouragement, my severest critic, my wisest counselor, my truest friend— Patricia Joy (Warren) Oldring, my wife.

VIII

GOING MY WAY

Joy and I met in England during the Second World War. I was a pilot in the RCAF. On one of my leaves I had stopped in Birmingham for just one day to see some of the fellows from our squadron. In some way I missed the fellows—but I met Joy. I was immediately attracted to her great beauty, but also to the person she was. I asked her if we could meet the next day, with no thought now of moving on as I had planned. We met early in the morning of that next day. It was October and it was raining. When I met Joy she was soaking wet. We had coffee and decided that a good start for the day would be to go to the theater. In wartime most things started early and finished early. Together we chose to see Bing Crosby in his film, *Going My Way*. It was beautiful. We have never forgotten the film and the theme song, "Going My Way," has become "our song."

Joy's home was in Bromley, Kent, on the outskirts of London, England. She and her mother had been evacuated from this dangerous bomb area, and her mother now had an important position in the Queens Hospital in Birmingham. Her father remained at his work in Bromley. Joy had only one sister, Audrey, who was a secretary in the Admiralty in London. She lived at home with her father.

Shortly after we met, Joy and her mother returned to their home in Bromley. I spent every leave visiting with Joy and her family. In between we wrote and phoned each other constantly. Before long we were engaged, and on the twenty-third of January in 1945 we were married in a lovely Baptist church in Bromley, Kent.

When the war was over I was sent back to Canada. Joy did not follow for seven and one-half months. It seemed like an eternity. Our reunion was wonderful.

Five children were born to our marriage. Edward Robin, now an ordained minister; Brian Warren, a medical doctor in practice in Calgary, Alberta; Margaret Ann, now Mrs. Smeaton, living with her husband, Doug, and two children, in Vancouver, where Doug has just completed his Ph.D. degree at the University of British Columbia; John Alan, an elected alderman in the city of Red Deer and a university student; and David Rodney, completing his high school at Mount Royal College in Calgary, after two years out in the work force and traveling through Europe.

How do you describe a marriage? Ours was and is filled with love, care and concern. Our daughter, Margaret, said it this way: after she was married and had moved to British Columbia, she wrote a letter to her parents that we cherish. This sentence was in the letter: "I want to thank you for the privilege of being raised in a home that was filled with love and laughter."

Our children were very much a part of the "love and the laughter," the "care and the concern." They are all loving people, and we not only cared for one another in good times and in bad, but we played together, we holidayed together, we laughed together with one another and often at one another.

Joy is a teacher and has twice been school principal, first in Ottawa and then again in Red Deer, Alberta, where she was principal of the Parkland School for Retarded Children. Joy has a gift with children. In Ottawa it was with the gifted children that she did some wonderful work. In Red Deer it was with the mentally retarded. In both Ottawa and Red Deer Joy gained the respect and the love of many people for her work with exceptional children.

One Sunday morning in Ottawa, I held the door of our car for Joy to alight prior to the morning service. Joy swung 'round and bent over to get out of the car, but when she tried to straighten up once her feet were on the ground, she could not. She was gripped with pain. She had slipped a disk in her back. It was the beginning of a long siege of back trouble that was to take her in and out of the hospital over the next nine or ten years. In Red Deer, in her third year as principal of the school, she developed a sudden case of asthma. She had not had any sign of it before. It was truly a sudden case. At times it could be very severe, and particularly in the very cold weather of winter Joy had great difficulty breathing. Like her back, her asthma was to send Joy to many doctors and into the hospital on many occasions.

Her own doctor in Red Deer told her more than once that she was going to have to give up her work. Finally, when she was in the hospital suffering from severe back trouble and asthma, her doctor said, "There is just no alternative. You must give up your work and take care of yourself."

He told me privately that it was most serious, and I would have to join with him in insisting that Joy stop work. I did not have to be convinced. I had felt sure this day would come.

Finally, reluctantly, Joy agreed and resigned immediately. It was January 1973.

At Easter of that same year, I took four days off and Joy and I went to Calgary. We stayed at the Calgary Inn and rested and talked and lounged and read. They were four beautiful days.

On the second morning when I opened one eye just slightly, Joy was not only wide awake but quite animated. It was apparent that she wanted to tell me something.

"I had the most beautiful experience last night," she said. "I wanted to wake you up and tell you about it. I almost did. I looked at you, but you were in such a sound sleep and I knew you needed to rest so I decided to wait until morning. I woke up in the middle of the night and for a long time I just lay there. I was thinking about all that has happened to us, then I prayed about it; I asked God to help me understand. The most wonderful thing happened. First a beautiful feeling came over me. It started right down at my toes, and it gradually came all the way up my body until I felt totally wrapped in a warm, peaceful—just the most wonderful feeling you could have. I felt perfectly secure. I just can't describe the feeling. It was wonderful. I felt close to God and I knew He was close to me. I began to pray again. I just wanted to thank God, but all of a sudden I was praying in tongues. It sounded so strange and yet it was beautiful. I don't know what language it was but I remember two words." Joy told me the two words and I recognized them immediately.

"You were speaking in Hebrew, dear, and the two words you remember are 'Holy Spirit.' "

Joy was not only uplifted but strengthened through this wonderful experience. Some years later, as we were going through the most difficult time of our ministry, Joy said to me, "You know, I don't think I could have gotten through this if it had not been for that beautiful experience I had in Calgary."

This experience was to have great significance for us, especially for Joy. She shared it with many people and many groups.

It was not the first experience she had received, nor was it the last. Others occurred later and some of them will be recorded in later chapters.

The first time Joy told of her experience was to our group in Red Deer. The second time was in the pulpit of Bell Street

United Church in Ottawa, our former pastoral charge. We had been invited by our former congregation in Ottawa to come in May 1973 and preach the services for their 100th Anniversary. It turned out to be a most rewarding experience. They had given me about ten months' notice and said, "Come and tell us something about the future. Give us some hope for ourselves and the church in the world of tomorrow."

It is my conviction that there is a lot of good news and reason for hope for tomorrow. I told them what I believe is the truth—that God is preparing to enter the world in a new way. He is preparing churches, congregations, ministers, laymen, for something much bigger than man's mind can comprehend. I tried to relate this new tomorrow to their church and their individual lives.

However, the reason I mention this part of our ministry now is this. We spoke at many gatherings besides the Sunday services, and we were entertained at banquets, lunches, teas—food constantly. We had gathered in one of the church halls to meet with and eat with a group of people before the evening service. The service started at seven-thirty. At exactly fifteen minutes to seven I leaned over to Joy and said, "How would you like to come into the pulpit with me this evening and tell these people about your experience in Calgary?"

"Oh no!" Joy exclaimed.

"Think about it, dear," I persisted, "don't decide right now." Silently I was asking God to lead us both according to His will.

As we entered the church shortly before the service was to start, Joy said, "I won't come into the pulpit with you now, but if I decide to come up during the sermon I will nod at you, and if I decide not to I will shake my head at you."

"Fine, dear," I replied.

Joy had come into the pulpit with me before. Other times she had had time to prepare. Not this time. There is another very important factor. Although Joy is a teacher, she is very shy and far too modest about her ability. She is in no way pushy.

I watched Joy through the service to see what her answer would be. Later she told me a part of this incident. She said that while trying to decide what to do, she was praying and asking God for guidance. Do you know what answer she got? "You have brains and ability; use them. Don't expect me to do everything for you."

I had already begun the sermon when Joy looked up at me and nodded "yes." At what seemed like the appropriate place I asked Joy to come up and tell her story.

The response was beyond even my expectation. After the service—at a social hour with more food—Joy was constantly surrounded by those who wished to talk with her, congratulate her, or ask her questions. Many simply threw their arms around her and hugged her. Some laymen from a church in Toronto asked her to be their guest speaker.

People were coming to me too. As I left the pulpit I saw my former secretary, a member and worker in the church, walking toward me smiling. She hugged me and said, "Something has happened to you, hasn't it?"

They did not want to let us go. But go we must. We had been meeting and speaking to groups now for five days. We had arranged for a week of our holidays at this time so that we could visit one of our favorite spots—Ocean City in Maryland. It was before the holiday season, so we were able to get first-class accommodation right on the oceanfront and at reduced rates. It was a wonderful week. In one of our evening prayer sessions together, Joy began to speak in tongues. It was the first time I had heard her praying in tongues, although it had occurred several times in her own private prayer life. It was strange at first but truly beautiful.

We had driven from Red Deer to Ottawa by car—a distance of about 2,600 miles. Before we left Red Deer my angels had shown me a number of scenes that would occur along the highway and had shown me that we would pass through fog along the Great Lakes. Every scene came true exactly as had been shown.

There was one addition. Coming through the fog in a very heavily wooded area the road twisted and turned; we were starting down a hill on a long, sweeping curve. Suddenly, out in front of the car, in the air, and right in my line of vision, I saw a red light. I instinctively slowed down, and right at the bottom of the hill as we came around the corner, I saw a single file of small school children being led across the road. They covered the whole road. At a reduced speed I had no difficulty coming to a gradual stop, and we watched the happy procession pass. There was no traffic light.

It was with some reluctance we said good-bye to Ocean City and began our journey home. It was an experience we will never forget.

In October of that year, back in Gaetz Memorial United Church, we celebrated Laymen's Sunday. Along with two other lay members of the church, Joy participated. She took the major portion of the sermon and as part of it told of her experience in Calgary. Again it was received with gladness and adulation.

IX

THE GROUP

Shortly after two of God's angels broke into my life, I started a study group in our home. I had always had study groups in my pastoral charges. Up to this time the work load at Gaetz had been so demanding that I had only scheduled short-run groups. It had always been my desire and intention to establish a once-a-week group. The work with the angels provided the stimulus to do it now.

The group started in my office at the church. I sent out a personal letter to a wide and diverse group inviting about fifty people to become charter members. Thirteen of us showed up for the first session. It was to be the smallest meeting we had. In two weeks we had outgrown the space at my office and we moved to our home.

We tried from the very outset not to be a select or an exclusive group. We announced the meetings in the calendar every Sunday morning, and we tried to indicate that the meetings were open and anyone could attend. We met every Monday evening and always a large group turned out. We sat on chairs, on cushions and on the floor.

Our meetings were scheduled to start at 8:00 P.M. People began coming by seven-thirty. Joy always had a large urn of coffee and a pot of tea ready with some cookies and sometimes cake or doughnuts. We only bought the coffee the first time. From then on there was always a pound or two on our kitchen table at the end of the meeting. Cake slices and light refreshments began to show up also. There was always something for everyone to enjoy.

Within a few months a core group had developed. Many came. Some occasionally; some for a short time. The core group was there all the time. There was an earnestness about the study, the prayer and the discussion. We were soon aware of a feeling of joy at being together, and a genuine concern for each other developed. There was always a happy air. Generally people did not come alone; those with cars arranged to pick one or two up and drive them to and from the meetings. From the moment people began getting out of the cars you could hear a happy chatter, and as they departed—usually after 11:00 P.M.—there was the same happy conversation, two and three talking at the same time.

From the first moment the members began arriving they gathered in small groups, standing with a cup of coffee in hand and talked together in an animated fashion. To start the meeting we would have to call people from three or four such groups. It was our custom to break again for coffee after about an hour. The smaller buzz sessions would begin again instantly. All who came found it a happy time, and almost everyone spoke of being "uplifted."

We began with a short prayer; we read the Scriptures, studied them and discussed them. We always had time for each to tell of special happenings through the week. Sometimes someone would have a special concern they wanted discussed. Each evening we had a prayer of healing. Usually we stood in a circle, joined hands and prayed for someone who was present and who requested a prayer, or for someone who was not present but for whom one of the group wished a prayer. Healings did occur.

There were other groups in the church and new ones sprang up every now and then. These too found interesting things happening. On several occasions I suggested to those leading the other groups that we all meet together once in a while to indicate that we were all of the same mind, spirit and intent. This did not happen during my time at Gaetz Memorial.

One Monday evening one of the regular members, Mrs. Maxine Gilliland, was limping badly when she arrived at the meeting. While little groups were chatting away throughout most of the house, Maxine sat back in an easy chair in a corner of the front room. I went over to her and said, "What's the trouble?"

"It's my back. I have a slipped disk and it is making my leg drag. My back is very painful, but I have no feeling in this leg."

Maxine was rubbing her leg and it too was bothering her.

"Would you like a prayer of healing with the group tonight?"

"Yes, I would, I was hoping that would happen."

When we had our prayer circle toward the end of the meeting, we often had the one for whom we were praying sit in a chair in the center. Some of us would place our hands on this person's head or shoulder. We tried to keep our hands joined at the same time. Maxine sat in the chair in the center, and some of us placed our hands on her head or shoulders, and we asked God in a very simple way to heal her. At the end of the meeting, when the little groups were chatting away for the third time, Maxine sat in the same easy chair in the corner. One of her friends, a neighbor, was standing near her. Maxine was still rubbing her leg, but she was smiling. She said, "The feeling is coming back. Oh, it hurts, but it sure feels good."

In a few moments she lifted her leg parallel to the floor without the aid of her hand and said, "I couldn't do that when I came in."

Maxine's husband, Fred, occasionally came to the meetings with her. Both were regular in their attendance at church (Maxine told me later that when she told Fred about the healing he was pretty skeptical).

On Wednesday morning of that week I was working away busily in my office when Maxine and her friend, Jean Halisky, burst in. They were too excited to worry about knocking. In they came, full of life and chatter. Maxine was healed and she pranced and turned and kicked to let me see she was healed. Jean said, "Isn't it wonderful? Isn't it exciting?"

I was jubilant too. But I had a different question. "What does Fred think about it?"

"Oh, he has to believe now," Maxine replied.

Whether this event was a turning point for Fred or not I cannot say. He did become a regular member of the group and a genuine friendship sprang up between myself and Fred. The Gillilands and the Haliskys are among our cherished friends to this day. We have been in touch with them continually. George and Jean visited with us from Red Deer about six weeks ago.

Later—almost two years after this healing—Maxine received a most interesting revelation. It concerned events that Joy and I were to experience. The revelation took form in a most unusual symbol. Maxine could not make head or tails out of it. I made an interpretation of the revelation, but I did not know whether it was right or not, so I did not tell anyone what I thought. It turned out I was right, and I hope someday to tell Maxine about it. That opportunity has not as yet come. It will. I will tell you about the revelation and the interpretation in a later chapter.

When the first summer holiday season arrived after the group had started, Joy and I assumed everyone would want to break for at least the two summer months of July and August. Not so.

"We won't all be away at once," they said. "Let those of us who are still at home meet."

This was the arrangement and not a single Monday night has been missed—not even since we left Red Deer. While we were still with the group we often had to be away on Monday nights. This made no difference. They simply met at other homes, and individual members took turns in leading the study.

It was a sorrowful group that said farewell to us. They gathered together two or three times for special farewells. They invited us to their homes to share dinners and evenings with smaller groups. They invited us to their homes as individual families. Nor have they let us go. They write, they phone. Just a few days ago a letter came saying, "Will you please write a letter to Ann? She is in need of an uplift." Ann is another member of the group.

This is not the only significance of the group in these days. They have constantly upheld us in prayer, and on at least two occasions they have received interesting and helpful revelations concerning the events that are befalling us all—but especially concerning Joy and myself. These revelations, like so many of God's messages and messengers, come in the most unusual ways. God does indeed move in mysterious ways. I will share two of these revelations with you in a later chapter. They have only recently occurred and belong in a different period of time than we are discussing now.

This is not an adequate introduction to the group, nor a sufficient treatment of the role they play. Like so many other aspects of this encounter with God, there is only time to tell some of the things that happened and are happening.

X

THE FALL OF '73

We had only nicely settled into the fall work in September 1973 when one of my angels said to me, "Ed, God wants to know if you are willing to give Him your church?"

I did not answer quickly; in fact, I was on the point of arguing the matter; yet I sensed a seriousness about the question. I simply said, "Yes, I am perfectly willing to place Gaetz Memorial United Church in the hands of God."

They answered, "Just to keep the records straight, you know, it never was your church."

Now I was prepared to argue. Throughout my whole ministry I had preached and maintained that the church did not belong to the ministers, nor to the congregation. It belonged to God. I am convinced that too often ministers and congregations alike act as if the church is theirs and often take such a stranglehold on the church that God and life are almost squeezed out.

We did argue, just a little. However, both the angels and I

knew my stand. There was something much deeper being introduced.

The Sundays rolled on. Laymen's Sunday was celebrated on the third Sunday in October and Joy preached her sermon. It made an impact not only on the congregation, but for a few days we were stopped on the street by people from other churches who wished to shake hands with Joy and congratulate her.

"We heard about your sermon and we want to thank you," many said.

That fall my hernia was particularly large and was giving me a great deal of discomfort. Finally Joy said to me, "Look, you have got to do something about that hernia."

I stood in silence. In my mind I was still convinced that God had given me that hernia and that He would remove it in His own time. An operation was not in my mind nor my plans. Joy seemed to read my thoughts. She was completely adamant. She said, "Are you going to phone Doug or do I have to do it?"

I phoned Doug and when he saw the hernia he said, "It has to come out, Ed. I'll get a bed in the hospital as soon as I can. In the meantime, if you have any trouble give me a call and we'll get you in through Emergency."

Hospital beds were at a premium, but by late December I felt there was an emergency, and the hospital called me in the first week in January to say a bed was available. I entered the Red Deer General Hospital on Monday, the seventh of January, was operated on the next morning, and on Wednesday celebrated my birthday.

I was not sick nor did I suffer any great amount of pain. A nurse gave me a hypodermic needle just before the operation and when I awoke in the recovery room offered to give me another. I declined and was back in my own bed shortly before noon. I was wide awake and decided that I was going to get out of bed and walk. I did. It was a little painful getting in and out of bed for a few days, but I stuck to it. I continued to decline the "hypos" and finally the head nurse came in and said, "Mr.

Oldring, don't try to be a hero. There is no need to suffer pain; we are here to help you get well without pain."

"I'm not trying to be a hero. Hypodermic needles make me sick. If I need one I won't hesitate to ask. Thanks very much. I'm really fine."

For the first few days I continued to walk up and down the halls. I simply wanted to heal quickly. The head nurse confronted me again in the middle of one of my strolls and said, "You are the most restless person I have ever seen. Why don't you rest while you have the chance?"

I was not to have the chance to rest for very long. On the morning of the third day after my operation a nurse came to my room and said, "Mr. Oldring, there is a patient in room 288 who would like to see you."

I went immediately. It was the first of many requests from people in the hospital. Requests came from patients on other wards and other floors. People came from outside the hospital with a variety of needs. Many came just to visit and wish me well.

Whether Dr. Doug was aware of this demand or not I do not know. After one week he came to my room late one evening and said, "Ed, you have got to get right away from Red Deer and give yourself a chance to get your strength back. I don't want you to think about going back to work for at least one month. Is there somewhere you can go?"

"Yes, we can go out to our daughter's home at Vancouver. Will you write a letter to the church board and tell them what you have told me?"

Doug was on the board himself; so was his wife. He wrote the letter and Joy and I arranged to visit our daughter. We spent a few days at home before leaving. According to Doug's letter, we were not due back until the twelfth of February.

We traveled by train through the Canadian Rockies. The weather at the coast was lovely. We walked every day and soon we were walking several miles. By the end of January plants were popping through the ground and buds were breaking out on the trees. It was delightful, and in my mind I kept hearing a voice say, "I hear you are going to Vancouver."

There was no sign of it as yet.

We stayed with our daughter and son-in-law for two weeks. We left Vancouver on the last day of January, a Thursday, arriving home the following day. It was about six-thirty in the evening when we arrived at our house.

We had not been home a half hour when the phone rang. It was our friend Bob Millar. His tone was grave and he was obviously upset. He said, "I have to talk with you. It is something very serious."

"Fine, Bob. Can you tell me over the telephone?"

"No, I would rather see you and talk with you face to face."

"Would you like to drop over to the house this evening?"

"No, I think we should have complete privacy. Can you come to the office tomorrow?"

"Certainly."

"Let's say ten o'clock tomorrow morning."

Bob was in an agitated mood when he arrived at the office Saturday morning. He could not relax; he said, "I have some bad news, but I wanted to bring it to you myself and I wanted to talk with you in person." There was a long pause. Then Bob continued, "Mr. C. tells me that he has three letters with two signatures on each one asking for your resignation. He tells me that if you resign he will tear the letters up."

The person whom I will refer to as Mr. C. was a member of the congregation. The message as I have recorded it is word for word the message that Bob brought to me. Mr. C. has denied that the message was sent. It remains my firm opinion that this was both the exact message and the intent. This message had still not come through any official church channel. There were means to process such an opinion. These were all bypassed.

I thanked Bob and told him that I was not totally surprised. Bob felt some personal responsibility. I tried to reassure him that this was not so. I then told him that I wanted to talk to Joy before I gave him an answer.

"I'll call you tomorrow or Monday."

That evening at home, I said to Joy, "What do you think about my resigning at the annual meeting next week?"

"Oh no," she replied, rather startled.

"Let's think about it and talk about it again tomorrow."

Both Joy and I continued to think about it and we both prayed about it. I had not told her, as yet, of Bob's news. I had been anticipating a move from Gaetz Memorial United Church for some months. I continued to pray for guidance. The guidance I felt I was getting was that I should resign. I wanted as much confirmation as I could get, and Joy was always a most reliable source of guidance. The next morning Joy said to me, "I think you are right; I think you should resign."

Then I told her the whole story, beginning with Mr. X. coming to my office, and of the news Bob Millar had brought the day before about Mr. C.

She was most distressed with the news but a little irritated with me for not having shared it with her before.

"Why didn't you tell me?"

"Because I didn't want you to be hurt."

"You should have told me!"

"Well, I did what I thought was best at the time."

Joy was hurt—for me. The hurt was to deepen.

On Monday morning I was back in my office one week ahead of the date Dr. Doug had ordered. There was a great deal to be done. The annual meeting was only six days away. First, I phoned Bob Millar.

"Bob, I am going to resign. Would you be kind enough to communicate this to Mr. C., but, Bob, please tell him that I am not resigning because of any letters he has. I want him to know that I am not resigning to what in my opinion is a form of black mail."

Bob was subdued. All he could say was, "I'm sorry, Ed, I'll give him your message."

Later that afternoon, Bob came bursting into my office like the old Bob Millar—full of vim and action.

"I've had time to think about this thing. You don't have to resign. There is only a small group that wants you to go. The congregation doesn't know a thing about this, and if they did they would soon outvote the few that want you to leave. Let's fight. Let's take it to the congregation. You don't have to resign."

"Thanks, Bob, you are right, but you must remember that I am not resigning because of this group of people. I don't think we should go to the congregation. I don't want you to be hurt, and I don't want any harm to come to the congregation. I believe I have to go. Let's make it as easy as we can for the congregation."

Bob accepted, but he was not entirely convinced, and he was "drooping" just a little as he left. I didn't give too much thought to this conversation at the time; I would expect Bob to be solidly on my side. The next day, however, just before noon a second man came into my office. He said, "You don't have to resign, Ed. There are a lot of us who are willing to fight this small group. We know we can win. We can take it to the congregation and outvote them by such a majority that they will have to be silent."

I answered, "I'm grateful, and I thank you, but I'm afraid you would get hurt. I'm also afraid the congregation would be seriously damaged. My main point, however, is this: I feel that God is asking me to resign. I believe that this church is fully in the hands of God. I also believe that God is going to shake this congregation to its very foundations, and then He is going to remold it so that He can use it for His own purpose. I don't think we should fight, but thank you so very much."

It was some time after my friend had gone that I suddenly realized I had just witnessed the interpretation of one of my revelations. You will recall the revelation—a friend came up behind me as I was wistfully looking at a church from some distance. The friend who came and stretched out his hand toward this church, as if offering aid, had two first names, as in Billy Joe. I declined the assistance in the revelation indicating that the church was prickly and the prickles might be poisonous. I indicated that I did not want my friend "hurt." The friend withdrew.

The meaning was now clear. Two friends would come and offer help. I would decline their assistance first because I did not want them to be hurt. I would decline their assistance for I sensed something very damaging in the situation—a poisoning effect. Upon my gentle insistence, the two friends would reluctantly withdraw. It happened just as it had been shown.

On Wednesday of this same week, one of my angels, who had been relatively silent for a few days, said to me in clear English, "We want you to withdraw your resignation; don't resign."

This was good news. I called Bob Millar and said to him, "I have changed my mind, Bob, I'm not going to resign."

"I'm sure glad to hear that," he replied, and you could actually hear the gladness in his voice. Later that evening Bob returned my call with this message, "I gave Mr. C. your message, and he says to tell you that he now has nine signatures and that he can get more."

This threat was not upsetting to me, and I continued with my work until the next morning. As soon as I came into the office on Thursday, my angels said to me, "Put in your resignation now."

When I relayed this information to Bob, he said, "Don't tell me you have changed your mind again!"

"No, Bob, I haven't changed my mind."

Actually I was puzzled by these changes of mind on the part of my angels. Why were they doing this? It is only in the light of all that has happened that I feel I can understand. I now believe there were two reasons for these changes of mind. I expected to be moved from Gaetz Memorial; however, it was impossible at that time to know all that was going to befall me and my wife and family. I had been shown that I would be

moved to a new church. I had not been shown that there would
be a two-year interlude. The first thing that I now believe is this:
I had to know that it was God who was asking me to resign from
Gaetz Memorial. It was certainly not the congregation. Later
events proved beyond a shadow of a doubt that the congregation
wished us to remain. Second, I had to know that in resigning at
Gaetz Memorial I was not taking the initiative, rather I was
simply responding to the will of God brought to me through two
of God's angels.

By Friday morning I felt satisfied in my own mind that I
must present my resignation to the congregation. By then I had
also decided that it should be done at the annual meeting that
was to be held following the morning service on the coming
Sunday. I had prepared my resignation in my mind and now
wished to have it perfectly typed by the secretaries. I called them
both into my office—I felt they had a right to know of this decision
now firmly made. As I told them, they did not say a word. They
just sat there and cried. Finally, I walked around from behind
my desk to the back of their chairs and put one arm around each
of them and said, "Come on now, some things just have to be;
I'm afraid this is one of them."

In the letter of resignation I began by thanking the congregation for the love and the loyalty they had given to both myself
and Joy all through the years. I told them my decision was not
an easy one to reach and that I had not made it entirely myself.

By the end of the day the letters were completed and ready
to be presented.

XI

THE ANNUAL MEETING

Before entering the hospital I had arranged for the Sacrament of the Lord's Supper to be served on Sunday morning, the tenth of February, just before the Annual Congregational Meeting. The meeting was held in the upper hall, a large multipurpose gymnasium. At one end of the gym there was a stage; at the other end were two sets of double doors leading to a hallway. Across the hallway was my office. I had decided that I would submit my resignation to the congregation at this meeting, and that I would give them a brief résumé of the events that had led to my decision to resign. During the past three years—years in which two of God's angels had been working in my life with my full awareness —I had both shared much of my experience with the congregation and preached to them about God's ministry of angels. Mostly they had received this news with gladness. I mention this now for one special reason. I had told the congregation from the pulpit on at least two occasions that it was my belief that God would move me from Gaetz Memorial and in the not-too-distant future. I had anticipated this move through the past year and was quite convinced that God was now initiating the move. Thus as the annual meeting began I was quite calm. I was genuinely concerned about the congregation, and like so many things that were to happen, I was totally unprepared for their reaction.

The agenda for the meeting had been drawn up by the laymen on the church board. They had included near the beginning of the agenda a place for me to say a few words. One order of business that was to come up later was the selection of a committee to begin a search to find a new associate minister. The associate had not been replaced at my suggestion. I had said to both the board and the congregation that before calling another minister a study of the type of service the church should be rendering in the community should be made. The study had not been undertaken.

In my letter of resignation I told the congregation that one of the reasons I was resigning at this time was to clear the way for them to search for two ministers who could work together and begin their ministry at the same time.

When my turn came to speak I held my letter in my hand and told the congregation it was my resignation effective the last day of June of that year. In our Communion that date is the end of the pastoral year and the time most ministers move. Very briefly I told them of the visit to my office of Mr. X. and the two messages that had greeted me on my return from a period of recovery following major surgery—the two messages sent by Mr. C. I emphasized both my gratitude to them for their loyalty and the difficulty that I had faced in making this decision. I then presented my letter and took my seat once more behind the long front table where the senior officials of the church were seated.

The meeting continued and very shortly a member of the congregation was making a report in connection with his office. It pertained to the search for a new associate minister. In his report he made reference to my ministry and connected it with a section in our *United Church Manual* to which he referred only by number, quoting a section and paragraph. I recognized the reference immediately. It referred to false doctrine. I had been careful to bring a manual into the meeting and I turned to it now. I was sure that I could open the manual to the right page immediately. I had, however, picked up a manual that was not my own and I was having difficulty finding the page I wanted. I decided the best thing was to go to my office and get my own manual.

As I rose to leave I turned to this man and said, "You are quoting false doctrine. The congregation has a right to know what you are talking about. I'm going to get my manual but I will be right back."

Joy was sitting near the front in an aisle seat. As I passed her I reached out my hand to her. She took my hand and rose to walk out with me. The congregation began to applaud, then they stood—nearly all of them—and gave Joy and me heartwarming support. Then some of them fell in behind us. More and more joined in, and a very large percentage of the congregation followed us into the hall.

The scene that followed will live in our minds forever. They threw their arms around us. They hugged us; they kissed us. They cried without shame and without restraint. They repeated over and over, "We didn't know a thing about this. How could such a thing ever happen? Why didn't you tell us?"

We did not return to the meeting. The scene in the hallway continued for at least half an hour. Little groups moved off to hold private conversations in other areas of the building. Some left the church with tears still streaming down their cheeks.

In the days and weeks that followed our telephone rang almost constantly and our mail increased manifold. Many letters were from church members who had been at the meeting. They went something like this, and this is an actual quotation: ". . . when I left the meeting that day I was just too full of sorrow to speak to you. How would nine people cause such a thing? We love you, we need you—won't you please reconsider. . . ."

It was abundantly clear that the great bulk of the congregation had no idea that there was in their midst a small group of people working to secure the removal of their minister. It was equally clear from the actions of so many in the congregation who came to us, who phoned and who wrote, that it was not their desire that we leave. One more thing was to become clear—the members were hurt, deeply hurt. The hurt has not healed yet.

People continued to approach us, in the office, on the streets and at home. Three questions were asked repeatedly; the first two were "Why didn't you tell us?" and "Why didn't you take this matter to the church board?"

I have pondered these questions in my mind ever since, and wondered whether or not I had been in error in the path I chose. I don't think so. I did not tell people because I did not wish to widen the conflict, to put fuel on the fire. I did not go to the official board because it is a standard practice of mine not to use either the pulpit or the official board to expose or punish people who disagree with me. There are always people who do not agree with all you say or do. Some of these people come and tell you face to face that they do not agree with you. This is not cause to go crying to a board. I have always listened to these people. Sometimes we become better friends. Sometimes we find our convictions are equally strong although opposed, and we often gain a new respect for one another.

There was, however, a deeper point of view. I had prayed a great deal about the visit of Mr. X. and about his attitude toward me. I had asked God directly in prayer—only once—whether or not I should go to Mr. X. and discuss the subject of his visit with him. It was my own method and desire to do this. At the very moment I asked this question I received a clear, firm unmistakable "No." In answer to prayer I did not pursue my own inclination. Looking back, as I have many times, I remain convinced that it would have been an error to attempt to talk with Mr. X.

The third question, and it is not always a question, was "Do you honestly believe that God could cause something like this to happen?"

Sometimes, rather than a question, it is a flat denial that God could be involved in something that causes so much hurt.

My answer remains the same; "God did not cause this to happen, but He did not stop it from happening. I firmly believe that God could have stopped this from happening and He did not; to that extent He caused it to happen. I am convinced that God knew, before he sent us to Gaetz Memorial, that these events would occur. I was given sufficient foreknowledge to know that something was going to happen that would involve my leaving Gaetz Memorial. In the messages that were given to me to deliver to the congregation there was confirmation of God's love for His church and His intention to shake it and to remold it. I still hold the opinion that God has this church firmly in His hand. I hold the further opinion that God will not let this church go and that He cannot fully use it until some in the congregation let go of their hold and let God in." I have told all this to the congregation from the pulpit: I have expressed these beliefs in private conversation.

This still, in part, is my answer to the third question.

XII

THE PETITION

The Annual Meeting at Gaetz Memorial did not end with the benediction that year, rather something was started that was to continue with great intensity for several months and which has not finished. People continued to phone us, to write, to drop into the office and to our home. In the letters that poured in people poured out their hearts.

One man who came to the office was a Mr. Walter Ogilvie, an ex-officer of the Royal Canadian Mounted Police, and a man who was for the second time a member of a congregation to which I ministered. Walt sat down and came right to the point of his call: "Some of us feel it is not too late to straighten this thing out," Walt said. "The congregation so far has not had a chance to say a word. Many of us believe the congregation is behind you. What we want to do is circulate a petition for everyone to sign. We would like to have your permission to do this."

"I am most grateful to you, to all of you, Walt. I'm not sure that I agree that a petition is the answer. You see, I feel that I must leave."

We discussed the idea for some time but no decision was made. When Walt left it was quite clear that he was not willing to give up the idea of a petition.

Later that same week a second man, a Mr. Henry Lembicz, who, like Walt, was both a friend and a board member, came to the office. Henry too wanted to circulate a petition. To Henry I simply said, "It is not my place to tell you what to do, Henry, or what not to do. You must do what you feel compelled to do. For my part, I must say again that I have decided that I must leave, and if you decide to take a petition around please remember that no matter how it turns out, I don't think I can change my mind."

With that Henry left and I did not hear another word about the petition until early March. Before that date an event was to occur that would change the situation in regard to the petition.

That event had its beginning at a regular official board meeting held on the evening of Tuesday, the twenty-sixth of February. At the Annual Meeting my letter had not been dealt with. In the United Church it is to Presbytery that a minister must resign. I had submitted my resignation to the Red Deer Presbytery and sent a copy of this letter to the official board at Gaetz Memorial. The official board was to deal with the letter that night.

There was a turnout for the board meeting of just over fifty members. When my letter of resignation, handed down from the congregational meeting, was presented, Bob Millar moved its acceptance. We had arranged that he would. It was seconded, but when the motion was put to the meeting only a very few hands went up. I had asked the people to accept my resignation, and the chairman reminded the group of this. By now a new chairman had taken over from Bob Millar. The question was put to the meeting once more, and this time thirteen members voted to accept and three voted against acceptance with the majority not voting. One of the three who voted against the acceptance sprang to his feet immediately and said what so many were saying, "The members of the congregation have not had an opportunity to discuss this matter. I move that a congregational meeting be called and the people be given their right to say what they wish."

The motion was seconded but it was ruled out of order. There was considerable confusion at this point, a motion was finally formulated and passed calling for a congregational meeting to be held after the morning service on Sunday, the twenty-fourth of March, 1974. I was of the opinion that the motion was one that would permit the congregation to discuss the letter of resignation. When the minutes came out the motion read that the meeting would be called "to notify the congregation of Mr. Oldring's resignation."

March was a very cold month in Alberta that winter. There was a great deal of snow and a very cold wind that brought a chill factor making for a low, low temperature. It was difficult for anyone to function in this kind of weather, but for Joy breathing was next to impossible out of the house. We agreed that it would be best for her to go to our daughter's in Vancouver. I knew I would miss her presence, but at the same time I was glad to have her out of the turmoil of these difficult days. Actually there was no decision to make; her health was of paramount importance and I secured for her a private compartment by train. Joy was not happy about flying those days, especially over the mountains. She would fly if there was any urgency, but if it could be avoided she would go by train or car. This was just one more thing that was to see a dramatic change in the next two years.

By now the first week in March was over and the congregational meeting was just two weeks away. Henry Lembicz came into my office to say, "We have decided to take the petition around. We realize that you will not stay no matter what the result is, so we are not going to word it to ask you to stay."

I looked at the weather outside and the calendar, and to myself I thought, "Oh no!" To Henry I said, "Good, Henry, it is going to be a real tough job in this weather."

"Yes, it is," Henry replied in his usual unperturbed manner, "but there is quite a bunch of us, and we are going to take the roll of the church and divide it up among ourselves, and we are going to call only on the official members. We don't want to leave any room for criticism or doubt."

They did the job. They did it beautifully. The results were overwhelming.

Gladys and Henry Lembicz tabulated the results, but they did a great deal more than that. They wrote a long summary of what people said to those who called. Actually they had two petitions signed. One they gave to Joy and me and one they kept in their own possession. To us they also gave a written summary of what people had said, and they also gave us the church roll that was used showing all the people called upon.

I saw the petition on the Saturday before the congregational meeting. It was a moving moment. There were just not enough words to express gratitude to these people who had tramped through snow and bitter cold, and often in the evening after a day's work had been done, to call upon nearly every home in a large congregation. Although I saw the petition the day before the meeting, their plan was to present it to me during the meeting.

The petition was a handmade document measuring fifteen inches in length and nine inches in width. It had a hard green cover with twenty-four sheets the same dimension as the cover; most pages were filled completely with signatures. On the cover in fairly large gold letters were these words: "OUR LOVE TO THE OLDRING FAMILY."

At the top of each page these words were typed in capital letters: "WE, THE UNDERSIGNED, APPRECIATE AND WISH TO DECLARE OUR CONFIDENCE AND FAITH IN REV. ED. OLDRING IN EVERY ASPECT OF HIS WORK AND MINISTRY IN GAETZ MEMORIAL UNITED CHURCH."

After seeing the petition I pondered in my mind whether or not I should reconsider my resignation. I had believed the members of the congregation were behind me; I had not dreamed that so many felt the way those who had circulated the petition said the great majority felt.

Early on Sunday morning, very early, Bob Millar phoned. "Ed, I have been up for over an hour praying about this meeting, and I feel that the answer to my prayer is that if the meeting asks you to stay you should."

"Thanks, Bob, I'm glad to hear that. I will be very pleased if the people this morning do ask me to stay."

I too had been praying and I felt that I had gotten much the same answer as Bob, but it was not clear.

The gym was packed to capacity for the meeting. I had remained at the door shaking hands with those who were not staying. When I entered the gym there were no seats left, and even standing room was at a premium. I remained at the very back of the room and sat on a table against the wall.

Among the first to speak was our friend Henry Lembicz. He spoke gently and quietly. It was a sharp contrast to previous times when he had spoken with great force and feeling. In one hand he held the petition. Henry covered the events of the last few months expressing clearly his own understanding of these. It was not until the final moments of his talk that he held the petition up and told of how it came into being. At this point it seemed to me that many people were talking and there was distraction. I could not hear what Henry was saying about the petition, and my feeling was that it was not the effective instrument that it might have been.

Others spoke, but my own reaction was that the meeting was not taking on any definite form. Finally Fred Gilliland stood up and moved, "that Rev. Oldring be asked to withdraw his resignation."

The chairman immediately declared this motion out of order. It was, however, seconded by Mrs. Catherine Mariott, and a heated discussion followed regarding the legality. The new executives seemed to have prepared both for the meeting and the motion that was now before them. They had asked Presbytery

to have an official representative at the meeting. Presbytery had
sent an official of the Alberta Conference, an ordained minister
who was a colleague and friend of mine. He was asked for a
ruling and stated the motion was out of order. He had not spoken
to me before the meeting and we talked briefly when it was over.
I asked only one question, "Why did you say that motion was
out of order?"

"Because I was told to say that," he replied.

I realize now that I should have asked him who it was that
told him to state such a motion would be out of order.

So far I had remained silent and right in the background. I
had watched the meeting with some astonishment. I felt now that
I must put an end to all doubt and deliberation. I received firm
confirmation as I made this decision. On my way to the front of
the hall my angels spoke to me in clear English, "Ed, you came
in peace; tell them to let you go in peace. You have ministered
to this congregation in love. You have kept faith with God and
with these people."

I thanked them and then I turned to face the congregation.
The sight that met my eyes is one that I have never seen before,
and one that will never fade from my mind. When I looked out
at the front rows of seats I saw, looking back at me, about
eighteen to twenty faces—ashen white. They seemed to me to
glare in hatred, and there appeared to be a hardness in the trace
of a smile, the set of the jaw and the lines in their lips. Looking
out a little further, I saw faces with genuine love and genuine
sorrow. Mingled with these were one or two faces with an expression almost of satisfied amusement, as if to say, "We told
you so."

I felt no anger and no hurt. God through His angels stood
beside me. I looked at the faces in the front rows again and
wished they were my friends. Some of them had been.

I addressed my first words to those who had worked so hard
with the petition and in other ways to try and keep me in Gaetz
Memorial. I thanked them all with all the gratitude one can

express in words. I thanked the people once more for their love and loyalty. Then I said, "I ask you, please, release me, let me go in peace."

To the whole assembly I spoke the words given to me by my angels. Then I added these words, "There is a dishonesty about this meeting. There is a lack of honesty about this whole proceeding. I beg you to be honest with yourself. I urge you to be honest with God."

Fred Gilliland, with the consent of the seconder, then moved to have his motion withdrawn. It was agreed. My resignation stood. The meeting soon ended.

Later in our home I phoned through to Joy in Vancouver. She was awaiting my call. After we had exchanged greetings, she asked anxiously, "How did it go?"

"Honey, you would have to be there and see it to believe it. Never have I seen a situation so thoroughly controlled by the Holy Spirit. We had them outvoted by a tremendous margin. And you should see the petition. But do you know what? We didn't make one dent in their armor."

XIII

NOT YET

It had been a morning I would never forget. After talking with Joy I made a cup of tea and sat down in my recliner chair. I pushed the rocker back so that I could stretch out with my head and whole body lying against the cushion, and I said out loud, "My ministry at Gaetz Memorial is over."

Quick as a flash two words were spoken to me, "Not yet."

Three months remained until the end of June. At the moment we had nowhere to go. I was still convinced that God would move us to a new church, and I felt sure it would be in Vancouver and at the end of June. On the phone to Joy I had said, "Our ministry at Gaetz is now officially ended."

Joy had answered, "Well, you had better start looking for a place for us to move to."

Later that day I spoke on the telephone to both our elder sons. Robin, our eldest, in particular said, "Dad, you had better get busy and look for a new church."

I did get busy. I phoned and wrote to friends who were in

touch with churches that were looking for a minister or churches where vacancies were pending. I wrote directly to several churches that I knew were searching for a minister. In a few cases we entered into dialogue with pastoral relations committees. But no call came.

When Joy returned from Vancouver she began immediately to pack our belongings. She felt sure we were going to be left without a church, and, of course, we had to be out of the manse at the end of June. I still felt a call would come. It was not until the end of May that I realized Joy was right. We had entered into conversation with a church in the interior of B.C. Things seemed to be going along well and moving quickly. This church had sent four people from their pastoral relations committee to Gaetz to attend a morning service. They had met and talked with me in my office after the service and then came to our home to meet and talk with Joy and those members of the family who were then at home. They stayed with us most of the day and before leaving invited us to their city for the next weekend and I was to conduct services. As they left our home one gentleman turned and said some very kind things to me and ended by saying, "Don't worry, everything is going to be fine."

On the following Saturday afternoon we met with the whole pastoral relations committee. Things seemed to be going very well, when suddenly late in the afternoon one man said, "I don't think we should make a decision just yet."

It was agreed that the final decision would be postponed. When Joy and I left the city on Monday morning, we both knew that we would not get the call, and I realized that we were going to be left without a church. By now our family and friends had come to the same conclusion.

In my study on Tuesday morning I sat contemplating what lay ahead. To my angels I said out loud, "God wouldn't leave us without a church, would He?"

There was a strange silence. It was complete confirmation. I then said, "Yes, I guess He would."

There was one month to go. I got busy and joined Joy in packing and looking for someplace to store our furniture, and someplace for Joy and me to move to.

Looking at things as they appeared that June of 1974, for Joy and I they did not look good. Things as they appeared were not the whole story. Joy had but one sister, Mrs. Audrey Mac-Kinnon, who was living with her husband and a son in Australia. Audrey's only daughter, Margaret June, had come to Red Deer for a visit and stayed to marry a very fine young man whose family owned and worked a very large farm just southeast of Red Deer. Joy and Audrey had seen each other only once since Joy moved to Canada and Audrey to Australia. For at least two years Audrey had been working and planning for a trip to Canada to see her daughter and her sister. She was to arrive late in the last week in June.

Joy and I had discussed the possibility of asking Audrey to postpone her trip for one year. We decided not to. After all, Margaret June was in Red Deer, and we could not say where we would be in one year's time.

One evening when Joy and I were busy packing, Joy suddenly stopped and said to me, "You know, I can see the hand of God in all this; I couldn't for a long time, but I'm beginning to see the pattern!"

I was delighted to hear this from Joy. So many of our friends were just not able to accept that God could be involved in such a difficult situation. Joy and I talked about it for a while; then our minds turned once more to the difficult decisions that must be made: where would we store our furniture? Where would we live?

Many offers were being made, both for storing our furniture and a place to live. "Come and stay with us," our friends were saying. "Stay as long as you like."

The offers were genuine. Joy and I had to attempt to fit the temporary into some kind of a permanent pattern. It was far from easy to see too far ahead.

We finally decided to accept our eldest son Robin's suggestion to store our furniture in the manse where he and his wife, Bonnie, lived. "Just as soon as you find a place we can send your belongings to you," he said.

Finding a place to live was complicated by the fact that we felt we should leave Red Deer, but we wanted to be close enough to visit with Audrey.

The end of June was fast approaching. We were doing a good deal more than packing. Invitations to visit our friends in their homes were pouring in. When we had no more dinner times that were free, people began inviting us to lunch. When all our luncheons were booked, people invited us to breakfast. People came to the manse every day—some to speak with us briefly, some to bring letters and cards with messages of thanks and farewell written inside. Many brought gifts. Some who came to the home and to the office just threw their arms around us and wept. And some who wept were strong men.

In other areas different things were happening. My angels were giving me messages that were to be included in sermons to the congregation. On one or two occasions they gave me complete sermons. Sometimes they left the sermon completely up to me. At times as I sat at my typewriter pondering the message for the Sunday sermon, my angels would say, "Ed, God wants you to tell the congregation. . . ." And the message would come.

Life was very hectic. We decided that we could not leave the moving of our furniture to the last moment. It was agreed that we would hire a U-Haul truck and take our belongings the ninety miles to the home of our son and daughter-in-law, Robin and Bonnie. Many laymen came to help. Fred Gilliland was the straw boss and organized the loading of the truck. We started fairly early in the morning and shortly after lunch the truck was ready to roll. Our third son, John, and our youngest son, David, along with myself drove the truck to Castor, Alberta, where our son Robin was a minister in the United Church. John did the actual driving; David and I were just passengers.

When it was time to unload the boys would not let me do any lifting. They did it all and we were back home early in the evening. Some furniture was left in the manse. Not much. Mostly we described these days as "camping," and we often entertained sitting on the floor.

Like so many of the areas in our adventure with God, it is impossible to adequately describe all that was going on in these hectic days. For instance, there was another group of people coming to the office to see me—some of those who had worked against me. The terminology "worked against me" is their own, not mine. For example, one young man, a man in his early thirties, came to the office and he said, "A group of us have been working against you for several months now, and I have been one of them. I want you to know that I am thoroughly ashamed of myself. Can you forgive me?"

"I knew that you were working against me," I replied. "I have already forgiven you. I have said so from the pulpit and I have said so in my prayers to God."

We talked for quite a while; we shook hands, we prayed together, we embraced. We parted in good spirit.

Others came and said much the same thing and we felt better for it. Some said, "I didn't know whether to come or not. I'm glad I did."

Not all who "worked against me" came.

Our friends in the congregation were planning a farewell gathering. It was to be on a Sunday evening one week before our departure and would be held in the lower church hall. I was preparing my sermons with care and in more detail than was usual for me. On that Sunday morning there was one sentence that I particularly wanted to say to the congregation. Normally my memory is good and I would have no difficulty including this sentence. This Sunday I was not willing to trust my memory; I enclosed the sentence in my sermon notes in a whole box of red ink and even underlined it in red. To myself I thought, "There, you can't possibly miss it."

But miss it I did. When the service was over it suddenly dawned on me that I had not spoken those words. I was rather distressed about it and a little puzzled. At the gathering in the evening I realized what had happened. Joy had prepared a speech for that occasion, and she had prepared it with great care and without any consultation with me and without showing me what she had planned to say. Suddenly, in the middle of her speech, out came the words that I had so desperately wanted to say. Joy said them beautifully and with great effect, and I knew who it was that had made sure I did not say them in my morning sermon.

Joy's speech was the hit of the evening. It was a kind speech. It was full of gratitude and acknowledgment of kindness shown to our family by the congregation. Joy had gone on ahead of me to Red Deer to get the children started in their schools. Her speech began by acknowledging the kindness of those who had met her at the railroad station and made her so welcome and done so much for every member of the family in their new surroundings. Her speech continued by recalling outstanding events and great contributions by the people of the congregation through the years. Joy was highly commended for her speech. Several people asked for a copy, and one man in making this request said he felt Joy's talk should be published and stated he would try to have this accomplished. One point I wish to make here is this: my deletion from my sermon of the words I felt were so important, made it possible for Joy to include almost identical words in her talk. I believe my omitting the sentence was not an accident. The angels of God do many wondrous things; they not only help us to say certain things, they also stop us from saying some things we plan to say. I believe my angels made certain that I did not speak this one sentence in my sermon for they knew that Joy would say it and perhaps with greater effect in her speech that evening.

At the close of the evening the congregation presented us with a beautiful tea trolley with an engraved plaque upon it, and a purse of money. Many individuals wished to present us with a gift of their own. Friends from former pastoral charges that we had served came to share that evening with us. Our family was all there too. It was a beautiful time.

Later our whole family gathered at our home. Together we lay on the floor or sat on the floor with our legs crossed. Together we counted the purse of money. It was just over fifteen hundred dollars.

The following Sunday was my last in the pulpit at Gaetz Memorial. When I had shaken hands with the last departing member, I turned slowly to walk to my office where Joy was waiting for me. Partly out loud and partly under my breath I said, "Now, my responsibility to Gaetz Memorial is over."

Once more my angels spoke two words to me, "Not yet."

XIV

IN BETWEEN

On the last day in June, Joy and I loaded our personal belongings into the trunk and back seat of our car. It was a beautiful, sunny day. We had kept back to take with us a small portable television, our golf clubs and, optimistically, I had set apart to travel with us my clerical robe, a briefcase full of worship resources and a small suitcase of sermon material. It was mid morning when we turned for one last look at what had been our home for the past nine years.

We had accepted an offer from friends to live for two weeks in a trailer spotted about thirty miles south of Calgary. We stopped in Calgary for lunch, browsed around the shops for a while, then, with unspoken reluctance, set out for the trailer. It was more than adequate in every way, but neither of us made any move to take anything from the car. Robin and Bonnie and their two children were going to Banff that same day in their converted school-bus-camper to begin their holidays. Brian and Jane and their two small children were planning on spending a day or two with Robin and Bonnie in Banff, and then going on for a holiday trip to eastern Canada and to our favorite spot in America, Ocean City in Maryland. The boys had suggested that we join them in Banff for a few days. Late in the afternoon, Joy and I looked at each other and almost simultaneously said, "Let's go to Banff."

In an instant we were in the car and on our way. By the time we arrived it was dark, and we were not sure we could locate Robin and Bonnie—and we were exhausted. "No Vacancy" signs were flashing everywhere as we looked for a place to rest for the night. We finally found a "Vacancy" sign and took a suite of rooms that was both large and expensive. Two couples stood behind us ready to take the suite if we declined. We slept soundly and awoke refreshed. In the daylight we were not long in locating our son's large red and white school bus. There was a warm and emotional hug all around. We were home again.

Later that same day Brian and Jane arrived and everyone of us decided to change our plans. Robin suggested, "Let's all stay together for at least two weeks. We can take day trips, we can fish; we have lots of accommodation for everyone. We are not going to move on until you have to, Mom and Dad."

It was agreed and a few days later we phoned Audrey in Red Deer and arranged to have her join us. It was a wonderful and refreshing time.

Joy and I had arranged to take Audrey and her daughter, Margaret, and Margaret's husband, Tom, on a trip through the Okanagan Valley and on to Victoria. Our reservations began the seventeenth of July. On the morning of the seventeenth Brian and Jane set out on their trip to the east, Robin and Bonnie packed their gear and headed toward Jasper, Joy and I and Audrew squeezed into our car and started toward B.C. Once more we hugged all around and sensed the things that were unspoken. The in-between time had started.

Audrey was scheduled to leave from Vancouver on her return

flight to Australia on the last day of July. We had geared our holidays to end in Vancouver where we could see Audrey off. It was with heavy hearts we said good-bye to her. It had been a wonderful holiday. Audrey could not thank us enough. For Joy and me a heavy cloud had hung over the entire month. We could not see a silver lining.

Margaret and Doug had invited us to stay with them in their home on the campus of the University of British Columbia. It was much more than a port in a storm; it was the answer to our great need—somewhere to lay our heads. Margaret and Doug were wonderful. They were loving, considerate and kind. But Joy and I were like fish out of water. It was a gloriously hot summer and we spent time at the beach lounging. We could not, however, relax and we did not agree on what we should do.

Although we had been "out of work" for a whole month, it did not seem to me that we had been on a vacation. I wanted to take one or two more months and just relax. Joy could not agree. She felt we had two priorities ahead of a vacation. She wanted me to start looking for a job and for a place to live. When we left Red Deer we took stock of our resources. We had three thousand six hundred dollars in cash, made up of our last salary check, the gift the congregation had given us, and a few dollars from our savings account. We also had two thousand dollars in Canada Savings Bonds and a few shares of Alberta Gas Trunk. We took with us sixteen hundred dollars in traveler's checks, leaving two thousand dollars in our bank account.

Accommodations in Vancouver were very hard to find and expensive beyond comprehension. At that time I could not see that this was the direction in which we should move. I still felt that God would lead us to a new church. Joy had her own ideas and she began to move in her own direction. At first I did not know that she was applying for jobs. One evening the phone rang and the call was for Joy in response to a position she had applied for in Victoria. It was a good job in the Bishop Cridg Center, an Anglican church institution operated by a board of directors. They were looking for a director of Day Care Services and were very interested in Joy. The executive director was calling to set up an interview in Victoria. The day selected was in the middle of the following week.

My angels had been strangely silent for sometime. Early the morning after the phone call, just as I was awaking, they sent a very rapid communication into my mind. They said, "Joy will come very, very close to that job, but she will not take it."

I felt I should not reveal this to Joy but rather let her work the situation out for herself. I did want confirmation of the message so I told Margaret and asked her not to say anything to anyone about it.

The night before Joy was to leave for Victoria she took sick. She was very sick. Margaret and Doug recommended a doctor and I phoned and described Joy's illness, giving him some of her medical history. He prescribed treatment and said that if she did not respond to call him again. By 11:00 P.M. Joy was alarmingly ill and I called the doctor again. He said, "Get her to St. Paul's Hospital as quickly as you can. Take her to Emergency. I will meet you there."

Margaret and I had Joy in the hospital before midnight, and within an hour or so the doctor had stabilized her condition. He said he wished to keep her in the hospital a while. At 2:30 A.M. just before Margaret and I left the hospital I told Joy that I would phone the Bishop Cridg Center and let them know she could not keep the appointment. At that point she did not appear to care much.

In the morning I was not able to reach the executive director but left a message for him. I was as careful as I could be not to put anything in the way of another call from Victoria setting up a subsequent appointment. Joy was released from the hospital for the weekend. Up to that time no call had come from Victoria.

On Sunday morning, the second Sunday in August, Mrs. Doug Bodwell called from Red Deer to say that her husband had died and the family wished me to come back and conduct the service. As I spoke with Mrs. Bodwell I found myself in a dilemma; I wanted to be available to these people, yet I wished also to be fair to the new ministers at Gaetz Memorial. Finally I suggested to her that the most ethical way to approach the situation would be to ask the ministers if they would mind my coming.

"If they have no objections," I told her, "I will come."

Her second phone call was not long in coming. She said, "I spoke with one of the ministers, and he said that it would not be ethical for you to come."

The Bodwells were a large family and I could hear the members talking in the background. They had made their minds up that I was to conduct the service. I did not want to be a part of any controversy. I asked if I could call her back.

"Yes," she said, "but we are not going to change our plans. Please come."

I discussed the whole situation with Joy and Margaret and Doug. We tossed it around for a half an hour. The three of them agreed. They said, "You must go; this family is in need of you."

Thus it was decided, and we further decided that Joy would come with me and we would travel by car. I relayed this message to Mrs. Bodwell.

We began at once to arrange our belongings for the trip back to Alberta. Most of our possessions were still in the car. Suddenly Joy said, "Let's stay in Alberta. Let's phone the boys and ask them to start looking for a house or an apartment for us in Calgary."

"The same thought has been going through my mind," I replied.

We phoned to our son John in Red Deer to tell him we were coming and to ask him to tell the rest of the family in Calgary, and, "Please, all of you start looking for someplace for us to live in Calgary."

There is another factor that I have not mentioned to this point. We owned two poodles. Joy had brought the mother from England. She purchased her at the age of four months from a kennel that developed a beautiful strain of apricot color. We called this dog "Taffy." Taffy had delivered two litters of pups with eight in each litter. Margaret had claimed one of the pups for herself. She named her dog "Suzy." When Margaret left home Suzy stayed with us. Thus we have two dogs! One thing they cannot stand is to be treated like dogs. Like our furniture our dogs were stored at Robin's house. Joy missed them very much.

We did not drive hard. We had told the Bodwells of Joy's recent sickness and had indicated that we would stop overnight on the way. We planned to stay in the apartment with our two young sons, John and David, while we were in Red Deer.

When we arrived they had a magnificent roast beef dinner all ready and a fridge filled to overflowing with steaks and all kinds of good food.

"We didn't want you two to go out and buy anything while you are here," they said.

By the time the funeral service was over, we were getting calls from many old friends—some inviting us to dinner, some saying to please drop in, and some requesting counseling sessions.

On the evening after the funeral, Joy said, "You know, I'm a little homesick for Vancouver already."

"I began to feel that way as soon as we passed through the mountains," I replied.

"So did I, but I didn't want to say anything."

The decision to stay or not to stay was not to be ours. We had not any more than finished this conversation when the phone rang. It was the executive director of the Bishop Cridg Center in Victoria calling for Joy. The man said, "We are convinced that you are the person for this position. We are prepared to offer you the job. Won't you please come and talk to us about it?"

It was agreed that we would return to Vancouver and phone Victoria as soon as we arrived so that an appointment could be set up.

Back we went once more through the mountains. John and David were most distressed at our leaving.

"We thought you would stay at least two weeks," the said. Their farewell was genuinely sorrowful. They agreed we had to go, but their countenance sagged, and so did ours.

In Vancouver we stopped at our daughter Margaret's home long enough to make an appointment in Victoria. Together we crossed on the ferry and found an apartment to rent by the month. Joy was not only offered the job, but they had already placed her name on her office door. She accepted and had spent half a day getting acquainted with her office and the staff. There was already mail addressed to her name awaiting her on the desk. It was the last Thursday in August. It had been agreed that Joy would start work officially the following Monday morning.

There were, however, other events occurring in our life that were paralleling these and which were to change the course of our personal history once more in these, our "in-between days." I will share these events and their outcome with you in the next chapter.

XV

THE RANKS
OF THE UNEMPLOYED

By the end of the first week in August in 1974 two things had become clear to us: we had to have some source of income, and we had to find someplace to live. During most of my years in the ministry ministers could not contribute to unemployment insurance and thus were not eligible to draw these benefits. This had changed in the last few years. We were compelled to contribute and thus eligible to draw benefits. Many people had advised me to take advantage of this. "You have contributed to it, Ed, you are entitled to the benefits."

I was very loath to do so. Still something had to be done. Finally I decided that I would go down to the unemployment insurance office and make inquiry. I dressed as I would for a working day—a shirt and tie, a jacket—located the building and walked in. I found myself in line behind three young men dressed very casually in the fashion of many of today's young. The lady behind the desk was neither young nor old. She spoke rather abruptly to these young men and directed them rather sharply using a pencil to point to various doors they must go through or signs they should have read. Then it was my turn. Her countenance softened and her voice changed; she even had a trace of a smile. She said, "What can I do for you, sir?"

"Something, I hope; I'm unemployed."

"Ohhh!" It was not a word, it was an exclamation. "Oh."

She was most pleasant and most helpful and told me far more than she needed. She showed me where to get registration papers and said, "Don't fill them in there. You will have to take them to the third floor and see a counselor, but fill them in as you sit and wait; it will save you a lot of time."

It did, and the counselor was also most helpful. But I heard some new words, "Do you have a separation slip," she asked.

"No, I don't; what is a separation slip?"

"Your employer should have given you one when you left; it is his responsibility. By law he must provide one for you within ten days. You can't even apply for unemployment insurance without it. However, I'll take your application and you write and get your employer to send you a separation slip."

To be entitled to unemployment insurance benefits you have to say why you left a job. You must write a little essay giving your reasons. I did so and handed it to the counselor. She read it and said, "If that is the only reason you quit, they will not start you on unemployment insurance until the full penalty period has expired."

I told her the story briefly; we changed the essay; they started me on unemployment insurance with the minimum required waiting period. The date of my first interview was the ninth of August.

There are other requirements for those who draw unemployment insurance. You are required to report to Canada Manpower

Center and register and be available for work. I did so. I went, as directed, to the manpower center at Howe Street in downtown Vancouver. They too were very helpful, although in the beginning they said, "What are we going to do with an unemployed minister?"

They referred me to the professional section and a counselor there became very helpful. I decided simply to tell her the story as closely as I could; that is, all that I told her was true, but I did not tell her everything. She said to me, "We have a job coming up at the Howe Street Manpower Center in mid September. They are interviewing people for this work right now. The only thing wrong with it is that it only lasts three months. Sometimes they keep you on longer than that and sometimes in the three months you can find another job. You meet a lot of people in this work. I'm going to put you down for an interview."

She made the appointment and showed me from her window where the building was to which I was to go. I kept the appointment. They were hiring sixteen people to work as project officers in the local initiative program of the federal government. They were interviewing some seventy applicants, and they would let me know whether or not I was successful.

While this was going on I received my separation slip from the treasurer at Gaetz Memorial United Church. There is a space that says, "Reason for Leaving." In this space were recorded two words, "He quit."

At the end of August I received my first unemployment check. It was for one hundred and five dollars. It covered one week. I was to receive two more: the second for two weeks and a third for one week. Then I was off unemployment insurance.

Getting an unemployment check is one thing; cashing it is another. I was to learn of the difficulty, the indignity and the embarrassment of presenting an unemployment check to a bank cashier. In the first place the envelope the check comes in and the check itself have large red letters announcing to all, "Here is an unemployment insurance check." The first bank I presented this check to just simply refused to cash it. Others said, "Take it to your own bank."

One young lady gave me quite a lecture. She said, "Why should you get money like this, and why should I have to pay the government to give money to you?"

I did manage to cash all three checks and was most grateful for the assistance received. In time I even became rather glad that I had had this experience.

With this background I now take you back to Victoria where Joy and I had rented an apartment and where Joy was preparing to start her work Monday morning, the second of September. The Bishop Cridg Center was actually looking for two people. Not only had the position of director of Day Care Services become vacant, but the executive director had also resigned and moved away. I spoke to one of the board members, and he seemed quite interested in the possibility that I might fill this position. He would take it up with the board. On Thursday, the twenty-ninth of August, Joy had spent half a day in her new office, and on Thursday evening we were to have dinner with the treasurer of the board. We were sitting in our apartment about 6:00 P.M. reading the "houses for sale" column, when the phone rang. It was a senior official from Job Creation Branch in Vancouver offering me the job for which I had been interviewed. "I'm sorry," I said. "We are living in Victoria now, and I won't be able to take the job."

"What is it?" Joy asked.

"Just a moment, please," I said to my caller; then putting my hand over the mouthpiece I said, "It is that job in Vancouver."

"Well, take it," Joy said.

"What?" I exclaimed. "What about your job?"

"Tell him you'll take the job."

"I'll be glad to accept the job; I'll be there on Monday morning, the sixteenth of September."

After I had put down the receiver, I asked, "Now what's this all about?"

"Well, I think it is more important for you to have a job than me, and I think now that I would sooner live in Vancouver."

That evening at dinner we had to tell our host of this turn of events. It was not pleasant, but like so much that had happened to us lately, it was something else that had to be. We explained that it was better for Joy not to start than to start and then have to leave her work, for I said, "I'm sure that before too long I will be going back into the church somewhere."

The board was very understanding but most sorry to lose Joy as its director.

On Friday morning we were off again to the ferry and back to Margaret and Doug's. They laughed as we returned. Margaret said, "We didn't disturb anything. We knew you would be back."

XVI

A MIRACLE BEGINS

As soon as we had returned to Vancouver we began in earnest looking for somewhere to live. If we found an apartment it would exclude the two poodles, but, then, could we ever hope to find a house in Vancouver that would permit dogs? Our intention was to rent, not buy. Not only could we not afford to buy a house, but we were not settled for anymore than three months— not as far as we could see.

One evening we took stock of what it was we were looking for. We preferred a house over an apartment; we did not want a lease, but a month-to-month rental; we wanted a house that would permit us to have our poodles with us; we had decided a fireplace was one of our priorities. We showed this list to Margaret and Doug. Margaret wasted no time, she looked at it, tossed it down with disdain and said, "Forget it, there is no such house in Vancouver."

In a more realistic fashion we began looking for a house, or an apartment, of any description. For nearly two weeks our search was in vain. Friday night, the thirteenth of September, Margaret and Joy decided we had wasted enough time. They said we had to go through House Hunters or Time Savers, both organizations which charged a fee and were supposed to help you find a house. The only help, as far as I could see, was that they gave you a listing of housing available before the newspaper came out. It at least gave you a head start. I made a bargain with Joy and Margaret. I said, "Give me until Mondy morning. If we don't have anything by then, we will go through one of the agencies." It was agreed.

In the paper Friday night we saw and marked two houses that were for rent. One said they were looking for a Christian couple. The other said it was a lovely white bungalow with two bedrooms and a fireplace near Queen Elizabeth Park. At the first house when we phoned there was no answer. It was the same at the second house. No answer on Friday and no answer on Saturday: we had made no progress. Joy suggested I phone the white bungalow number Saturday evening. I did and got the owner immediately. She said that many people had already answered her ad and that the first two couples were coming over the next day, Sunday, to look at it. I said, "We will come over right now, if you wish."

"You wouldn't have me do that would you?"

"No, I wouldn't. I was only expressing my own desperation."

"I'll tell you what I will do. I'll put you down as third on the list; if the first two couples turn it down I'll give you a call. But you won't hear from me; the first couple to see it will take it."

On Sunday morning when we awoke, I had made a decision. So had Joy. My decision was to phone the house that was advertising for a Christian couple. Joy's decision was more serious. She said, "I think I will go back to Calgary and stay with Brian and Jane for a while. I don't think I can take much more of this."

I couldn't argue and I didn't. Nor did I try to dissuade her.

It had been an ordeal beyond description. It was obviously far from over. I simply said, "O.K., dear."

I went ahead with my plan to call the first house.

I timed my call for just before 10:00 A.M. They had stated they wanted a Christian couple, therefore, I concluded they would be going to church but would not have left yet; still they would be ready to go. That was a time schedule I knew fairly well. I realized there was a calculated risk at phoning on Sunday. The risk was even greater that by Monday it would be too late. All went well. They were charming people on the phone and seemed pleased at the prospect of a minister and his wife being in their home. The rent was also the lowest we had heard—two hundred and thirty-five dollars per month. They said they would hold the house till 1:00 P.M. Doug and I immediately got in my car and drove over to see it. The house was small but it looked adequate, clean, but the street was crowded and there was not a tree in sight. More than that, it was very noisy. My heart sank. I said to Doug, "I don't think I could leave Joy alone in this area and go to work in peace."

We returned to Doug's house and just as we entered the phone rang. It was for me. It was the lady who owned the little white bungalow. It took a minute or two to understand what she was saying. She was angry but not at me. The first couple who had an appointment to see the house did not show up. The second couple hemmed and hawed about the size of the second bedroom. She had finally asked them to leave and phoned me. Now I could hear her; she said, "If you can get over here right away you can have the house."

"It will take me twenty minutes, but I'll be there."

I phoned the first people and told them we had found a house and thanked them very much for their kindness. They had already people on the spot wanting to rent their house. Doug and I flew out of the house and hurried to the address that had been given to us.

Doug knew Vancouver and was calling out the turns for

me so that I did not notice the address of the house until after we had arranged to move in.

The house was beautiful. It had a lovely rock garden and a good closed-in backyard with an apple tree and a cherry tree. It had a carport. In the house there was a completely finished downstairs. There were two fireplaces—one upstairs in the living room and one downstairs in the family room. As we approached, homes along the street were delightful and as soon as I saw the house I knew it was the answer to our prayers. In fact, as soon as we left Margaret and Doug's my angels said, "This is your house."

And it was. I saw the lovely garden, rushed through the house and said to the owner, "We'll take it."

"Wait a minute, you haven't seen it."

"Oh yes I have; we'll take it."

"A house like this deserves a better look than that; come on, I'll show it to you."

Once again we went through it. It was everything that we had listed and then some. It was no distance to the bus line and buses during the rush hour ran to the downtown area every five minutes. At the end of our street, four houses away, was Queen Elizabeth Park—a beautiful park to which people came daily from great distances. As we walked from the house into the garden the lady asked me if we had a dog. I answered, "Yes, two of them."

"Well, they will enjoy this garden, and as you can see it is fenced in." I had already seen. The owner said, "The rent is four hundred dollars a month, first and last month in advance."

I knew that too; it said so in the advertisement. I said once more, "We will take it; when can we move in?"

"You can move in on Wednesday."

The deal was made. I said, "Can I make a phone call?"

Wednesday was the eighteenth of September; that was Joy's birthday. It was Joy I wanted to call. When she came on the phone I said, "Honey, I've got a birthday present for you. We have a house and oh, darling, it is beautiful."

We were both thrilled and relieved, although the relief was forgotten in the joy of having found a house. And not just a house—a house that anyone would have said was unobtainable in Vancouver. There was no lease and the landlady could not have been nicer.

In the rush I had forgotten to bring any traveler's checks or our checkbook. We rushed back to get Joy and Margaret and our checkbook. Joy loved the house from the moment she saw the outside just as I had. We were both delighted. And then for the first time we saw together the street we were living on. It was Alberta Street.

It was a miracle, but it was not the end of the miracle; it was just the beginning. This delightful house was to be our home for one year and one month.

On Monday of that week I began my work at the Job Creation Branch of the federal government. The office I worked in was on the fourth floor of the Canada Manpower Center at Howe Street, where I had gone to register. As soon as I could slip away I went up to the seventh floor to thank the counselor who had directed me to this job.

On Wednesday we moved into our house at Alberta Street. It wasn't a big job. We had only the things with us that we had been carrying around in our car. Our furniture was still in Alberta. We bought a bed and mattress; there was a stove and fridge in the house, and we phoned Robin and asked him to arrange to get the furniture to us as soon as possible. One week later the three oldest boys drove the furniture out in a U-Haul truck. Doug helped us unload and then we all had a wonderful visit for two days before the three sons flew back to Alberta.

XVII

THE BUSINESS
WORLD

My contract with the federal government was for three months;
it expired on Friday, the thirteenth of December. Most of the
people in the Job Creation Branch were on temporary status.
Thus I was not the only one who scanned the employment page
of the Vancouver papers.

I had not been long at my new work when I saw an advertisement in the weekend paper for employees for the Windmill
Toy Stores. It stated they were looking for full- and part-time
workers. Mostly it appeared they were looking for sales staff
for the stores. It was a large ad and very interesting, but I
decided it was not an area for me to explore. A few days later I
saw this ad cut out of the paper and pinned up on our notice
board at home. Joy had answered the ad. She was soon called for
an interview. She said later it had been her intention to apply for

part-time work, two or three afternoons a week. As it turned out the Windmill Toy Stores had been taken over by a group of Vancouver businessmen and their intention was to expand. They were opening two new stores right away and were looking for two managers and a sales staff to include full- and part-time workers.

Joy was offered the position of manager at one of the stores. The smaller of the two stores was not too far from our house; the larger store was right downtown in Vancouver. Joy asked for the small store; they had made their mind up that she would be made the manager of the downtown store. She excelled in her relation with the staff and had a harmonious and successful store. This did not go unnoticed. Early in January she was promoted to the position of personnel manager for the company and moved to the main office. Through the year of 1975 six more stores were opened in Alberta, Saskatchewan and Manitoba. In every opening Joy was put in charge of setting the stores up and hiring the staff. During this time Joy was also working to establish a new area in the Windmill—a showroom to display toys and equipment to cover every need in the field of early education. In this area Joy had had a great deal of experience and had become most knowledgeable. It was her goal to provide one location where all those engaged in early education could obtain every single piece of merchandise that might be needed. During these months she had been gathering information concerning all preschool organizations and education in the school system up to grade three. She had also been searching for suppliers of the merchandise these organizations would need. She had her own ideas about much of the equipment that would be needed, and where she could not find someone already producing such equipment she took drawings to new local sources and said, "Could you make this kind of equipment? How fast can you turn it out? What kind of a price will you charge us for it?"

One spin-off from this kind of research was that Joy was now being introduced to the purchasing end of the business world.

Toward the end of 1975 she was promoted again, and her new responsibilities now included some of the buying for the fifteen stores then in existence.

In an earlier chapter I made reference to Joy's reluctance to fly. With the Windmill she has been flying continually. As I write this chapter she has flown to Europe on a buying trip that will keep her away from home for approximately five weeks. During that time she will fly to several cities and attend a number of toy fairs. She has now lost all reluctance at the thought of flying. Nor is this the only fringe benefit of her work: in opening new stores she had been lifting heavy packing cases and stocking shelves. She is now discovering new strength in her arms and in her chest.

Before the end of my first three months in the Job Creation Branch my work contract was renewed and extended for an additional six months. This process would be repeated several times, and I would be kept on in this same work until—nearly two years later—the call to a church, that I had been so sure would come, was to become a reality.

The Job Creation Branch was a recent innovation of the federal government. It was about four years old. Its objective was to reduce unemployment by providing jobs through a number of programs financed largely by the federal government. Much of our work was done outside the office. Thus we were assigned a territory somewhere in British Columbia and were placed on a travel status and had an expense account. It was actually a delightful job. When asked how I liked it, I would reply, "Well, if I have to be out of the ministry I find this rather a satisfying situation. I consider myself very fortunate to have found this work."

Much of our work was in direct contact with people—people who were willing to cooperate with the federal government in implementing programs to create jobs, and people who needed jobs and needed some kind of nurture to assist them in making their way back into the permanent work force. Thus there were many rewarding moments.

I found my fellow workers and the Canada Manpower personnel, who shared the same office building with us, both congenial and helpful. They were interested in the fact that I was a minister. I found an opportunity to look at life through their eyes. I heard their assessment of the church. I listened to their understanding and interpretation of ministers and religion. They spoke with great frankness and openness: they held nothing back. It was educational. Some sought out an opportunity for a few moments of private conversation to speak with me about their own problems, their own aspirations, their own lives. I was grateful for these moments but was very careful and deliberate in letting all the initiative for such times come not from me but from my co-workers.

From our office all the administration was carried out for all federal government Job Creation programs, and the implementation of such programs was also our responsibility. This often required that we be away from home for the whole week and sometimes traveled for two and three weeks at a time. This was largely a matter of personal choice. One factor I found interesting was the contrast in how the expense account for performing a job was paid.

In the ministry too often the cost of travel, the car allowance, was first of all just that—an allowance; that is, a part of the cost of operating an automobile was paid. Second, too often this was thought by the lay people to be part of your salary. In the United Church of Canada a car allowance was included in determining the assessment a minister must pay toward his pension. Other types of travel for the church are often subsidized. In the business world, when I traveled, an airplane ticket was placed on my desk, a "drive-yourself" car rental awaited me at the airport of my destination and reservations were made at a hotel or motel. Nor was there any confusion as to what my salary was or on what my income tax and pension contributions would be based. My salary was quite apart from the cost of performing the service being rendered. It was all a great revelation. Of course, it was not all one sided. My house rental was not a tax write-off. It was just a living expense that must be paid out of my salary after income tax and other deductions had been made. Thus I found myself paying more income tax than ever before. All in all, the business world came as a revelation and an education.

During these months the angels who walked with me were constantly at my side. Communication was not always at a level that I could appreciate, nor did I like all the things that my angels were doing. You will recall one of the visions given to me that I shared with you in chapter six—seeing myself as a football. As I looked at this sight, one of the angels said, "Ed, we are going to kick you all over the face of the earth."

They were still at it. An almost constant pressure was exerted on me. As the case had always been, there were intervals when all such activity and pressure would cease; there would be a beautiful peace. Such times varied in length; however, they did not last too many days. "The kicking around," the pressures—which were of many kinds—returned. I cannot pretend to know all the reasons for this type of treatment. It did force me to concentrate under most difficult circumstances. My ability to withstand the torment and the pressure increased. My resentment toward it modified. These are likely part of the purpose but not likely the whole of it.

Among the revelations given to me that I have already shared with you is the one where I was both shown and told that I would be placed "for a short time" in a type of solitary confinement. What I was experiencing in the business world and through the nearly constant pressures of my angels was a form of isolation. It was not only an isolation from the ministry, it was also a separation from my family. They could not accept my statements of the things that were happening to me. Finally I simply had to stop telling anyone, including my family, what was happening in my life. I was compelled to bear it alone. I did not attempt any longer to share these things with Joy.

I still believe that all these things were part of God's plan for our life. I believe that God placed both Joy and me under this tremendous pressure, burdened us in this way, to strengthen us and prepare us for service in a ministry yet to come.

Let me share one more rather important revelation with you. It occurred in Gaetz Memorial United Church in Red Deer on a February evening about four years ago, about two years before we left Red Deer. At ten-thirty one evening, when my day's work was finally finished, I was the only one left in the church. I turned out the lights in my office and made my way into the sanctuary and sat down in total darkness. I sat for quite some time in the darkness and silence. Then I offered a most earnest prayer to God. I told Him that I did not think I could bear much more of the torment. I told Him that I could not understand the reason for it, and then I asked Him in His goodness and mercy to remove the torment.

The first response to my prayer was that a great pressure settled over my body and pushed me firmly against the unyielding pew in which I sat. Then a spotlight, a round light about the circumference of a volleyball, began to flash high on the end wall at the back of the chancel, that is, the worship end of the church. The chancel did not have an outside wall. The light could not possibly have come from outside and hit that spot. At any rate there was no light flashing outside. Nor was there any visible source of this light within the church. There was no beam of light, just a spot on the wall flashing on and off. I then noticed that the flash of round light was coming with about the same regularity of a heartbeat. I simply sat in silence and watched the flashing light. Actually I could do little else. The weight, the pressure that covered my whole body held me firmly against the pew. After some time a voice said to me quite clearly, "Your burden will be lifted in time."

The pressure lifted. I rose in silence and went to our home. My mind still clings to these words; I do not, however, dwell upon them like I used to. The pressures continued, and my strength increased, and I can see more clearly the hand of God in even the most difficult of the things He asks us to bear.

In the Old Testament, Jacob said he had wrestled with God. I feel sure that most people in the world today cannot understand this. It seems to me that some people accept it as a fact without understanding it, or they refute it as a figment of Jacob's imagination. Of course, many people do not see it as in any way significant and give it little or no thought. Today I can understand it at least in part, for I have been wrestling with God. It is a most difficult thing. There are no rules. Sometimes a pattern seems to emerge and you think, "Now I am getting the rules."

Then the pattern changes again and once more you know "there are no rules."

You cannot do the right thing, that is, make the right response. Sometimes after your very best day's work the torment is the worst.

It is a test of faith. It is a strengthening of one's ability to concentrate under pressure. It is a test of your knowledge and faith in Scriptures and in Christ's teachings. For instance, at times I used to express great anger and resentment at my angels for some of the torments to my body. Then I could hear in my mind Jesus say, "Do not return evil for evil . . . do good to those who persecute you." If you work with God's angels you must try to learn to relate to all people in loving kindness. The attitude toward all must be an attempt to be creatively positive. Surely it is required that we relate to all people, so far as it lies in ourselves, in an attitude of peace and goodwill. In addition to this there is the requirement of getting yourself into the background. It is a tremendously high standard, and perhaps no human being can fully attain it. It appears that God is asking some of His followers to at least make a real attempt.

Thus when you wrestle with God it is He who initiates the contest. It will not end until He determines. Thus if you fall prostrate before Him in utter surrender, the match goes on; if you strike back in any fashion at your disposal, it makes no difference. God does not change His tactics.

Early in this encounter—and let me say only in my case— the wrestling was with God's angels. It could, however, only be with God's permission. Nonetheless, it was God's angels who did the wrestling. Early in this encounter I felt that the only way out was to terminate my life on earth. Since then I have pondered whether or not I was serious. I cannot say. Surely in the beginning I was desperate. I told my angels that I did not fear them for I knew that I was a child of God and under His protection and secure in the salvation of Jesus Christ. I said, "I am not afraid to enter eternity. I know where I have stood and for what I have stood. You can't keep this up forever. God will stop you one day, but if you don't stop it soon I am going to."

This in part is the isolation I have been in; this in some small measure is the torment to which I have been subjected and the wrestling match in which I have been engaged with two of God's angels.

Nor is this the whole story of these in-between years. There have been long and ever-increasing periods of truce when some real work has been accomplished. In one week, when I was traveling a long distance out of Vancouver, I went to bed early one evening for I had a heavy schedule of work lined up for the next day. In my travels I worked long hours so that I would not have to be away from home for more than one week at a time. For the following day I had arranged a tight schedule of work beginning before eight o'clock in the morning and covering a distance of more than one hundred miles. Before the call from the desk came to start my day my angels woke me up and said, "Ed, we are going to take you today where you do not want to go."

I had my own plans and I was not prepared to give them up that easily. I did not answer. I simply got dressed and ready for the day.

My first appointment was for breakfast in the home of a client twelve miles from my motel. I arrived a few minutes early, but my client and his family were awaiting my call, and breakfast was served immediately. When our business was completed and I was once more in my car moving on to my second appointment, I looked at my watch and noted that I was still ahead of schedule. By ten o'clock in the morning the business for the second appointment was completed and I rose to take my leave. My client, by now a friend, wanted me to join him and a few friends for a morning coffee. It was a pleasant break and the people I met were both gracious and interested in the work I was doing. One man in particular wished to show me a new business site he was developing. I didn't get an opportunity to accept or decline; my smiling friend took me by the arm and ushered me into his car and off we went. It was after eleven when I began to make motions toward my own car and protestations of my need to move on. My host said, "You can't go yet! I want to show you a really huge development just out of town."

I knew the area and it was thirteen miles away. I said, "I haven't time to go out there. I am already late for my next appointment."

"You can't leave now, Ed. I phoned my wife and she is expecting us both for lunch." Looking at his watch, he said, "We have just enough time to drive out to the site and back."

Off we went. At lunch I was asked to say grace. It opened up a conversation that lasted over two hours and led to an outpouring of a man and his wife and an inpouring of the love of God which was beautiful to behold. The needs of these people became very clear and the meeting of these needs by the Holy Spirit was equally clear. My next appointment? I phoned ahead and rescheduled the remainder of the day.

In this work I did not make it known that I was a minister. I had no reason to conceal the information. I knew that from time to time I was led to certain people and situations, but my place was to do the job I was given. For instance, I had spoken on the phone to a Japanese gentleman who lived in the interior of B.C. We had never met, but he had often invited me to stop in and see him if I was near. On one trip I had to drive through his town. I had done so before but this time I felt I should stop and say hello. I had appointments seventy-five miles further on and was anxious not to stop for long.

His secretary showed me in right away, and we chatted and then he asked me to stop in late that afternoon on my way back. I told him that I was not coming back that night. He insisted that he wanted to speak with me and finally said, "I'll wait in my office until five-thirty. Please try to be back by then; if you're not I'll know you're not coming."

I hurried through as much of my work as I could and did return to meet this man by five o'clock. We talked for a while; then he said, "When you came in today my secretary said, 'There is something special about this man. I think you should see him.' "

He asked me a number of questions; I answered them simply but directly. He then asked, "What did you do before you worked for the government?"

"I was a minister in the United Church," I answered.

"Oh," he said, with his delightful Japanese accent, "how come you left the ministry?"

"It's a long story. I don't really know how to tell it to you in a minute. You see, God gave me a gift of healing."

"Now I know why you have come; I'm going deaf. I can't hear on the phone anymore. If I get any worse I will lose my job. Will you heal my deafness?"

Now I had put my foot right in it. I couldn't heal his deafness, not unless God did it through my hands. Would He? I couldn't be sure. I knew one thing; for this man I had to run the risk of looking foolish. I had to do what I could and leave to God what I could not do.

"Will you have a prayer of healing for me right now," he pressed on.

"Yes," I said. "Come on, let's ask God to heal your deafness." He knelt down on the floor and I placed my hand on his head and in great simplicity asked God to heal his deaf ears.

We talked for a little while and then my angels spoke to me. One of them said, "Tell him that his healing will not be felt today. By tomorrow he will feel a difference and within five days he will be greatly healed."

I told him. He was sure it would happen. I asked him, "If you feel your hearing is better, will you phone and let me know?"

"I sure will."

Back in my office at the beginning of the next week I wondered about the healing. The phone didn't ring and I thought, "Well, I guess he wasn't healed."

It was two or three weeks later that I had to call him on business. When I said, "Hello, this is Ed Oldring spe. . . ." I didn't even finish the word.

"Ed, am I ever glad to hear from you. See that? I can hear you real good."

"Is your hearing really good now?"

"Well, you should know, you healed me."

He was so sure that there just wasn't any reason to phone and tell me. Then my angels told me something else, and I passed this message on. The man was still thanking me. This was the message I was given: "Listen, don't you thank me. Do you want to know who to thank? Thank your wife. She has been praying for God to heal your hearing. He answered her prayers." To this day the man still thanks me.

Through these eighteen months in the business world many things have happened. Many people have been praying and very earnestly for me. They know that I did not willingly or deliberately leave the ministry. Among these people is my wife.

One evening in the summer of 1975 Joy and I had gone out for dinner. We were sitting quietly, and Joy said to me, "What does a deep blue color in the aura mean?"

"Well, dear, if it is across the top—kind of flat—it means that you are a fighter on the side of God. Like Paul said, 'in the good fight'—it doesn't mean you are an aggressive person, just that you are in the fight on God's side."

"What does the color gold mean?"

"Well, again, if it is flat across the top, it means you are under the protection of God. Why do you ask?"

"A few mornings ago, after you had gone to work, I was in our bedroom praying for us—mostly for you—asking God if He wasn't going to lead you back to a church, and the whole end of the room was covered with a deep blue. It was flat and across the whole room. On top of it covering the whole room was a beautiful band of gold."

"It means, dear, that you and I are still in the fight on God's side, and we are still under God's protection."

Joy nodded. She was very thoughtful. Then she said, "Right in the middle there was a white cross."

"It means that it is not time yet for our burden to be lifted," I said.

Shortly before this, about three months earlier, a lady, a friend of ours from Red Deer, phoned; she was quite animated. She said, naming two ladies who live together in a beautiful home in Red Deer (both were members of the group), "The two of them were entertaining an Anglican minister's wife who was visiting in Red Deer. One night, just before they went to bed, they were having a prayer together. Suddenly the Anglican minister's wife began to speak in tongues. When they had finished the prayer the Anglican minister's wife said, 'Well, I don't know what this is all about, but I am to tell you two ladies that you are to tell the group that God says he has your minister securely in His hands and you are to stop fretting.' Then one of the ladies said, 'It's all right, we know what it means and it is good news.' "

These were just some of the things that were happening in the in-between time and during our time in the business world. Many more things happened—some good, some very good, and some most painful.

XVIII

AN ONGOING MIRACLE

On a sunny afternoon in June 1975, Joy and I were sitting in our garden chairs in the backyard. Joy said, "I wonder what is going to happen to us?"

"We will be out of this house by the end of October," I answered.

"Where will we go?"

"I don't know. We might not move until the end of November, but we will not spend another Christmas in this house."

Joy also appeared to sense that we were going to make some kind of a move. Her wish was to buy a home in Vancouver. She had a deep longing for a security greater than that which had been ours for the past two years.

Shortly after that conversation, she began searching the newspapers for houses for sale. We began to spend every weekend looking at houses. At first I felt that it was a wasted exercise. In my mind we were going to be moved "in the fall," and I was sure this would be the fall. I had convinced myself that the move would be to a church and out of Vancouver. We found the price of houses extremely high. We began to look at townhouses. These were nearly as high, and we soon realized that with a townhouse you do not own the land. To us it was not a sensible direction in which to move. We looked at duplex homes, in fact, at homes of every description and price range. It was a time-consuming and frustrating exercise. One thing it did was to give us a good feeling for the housing market in many areas of Vancouver.

In late August our search for a house was given a real incentive. Our landlady called to say that she was putting our present home up for sale. Once again we faced the prospect of being homeless. It was another shock for both of us. I tried to console Joy with the thought that houses were not moving quickly and we likely had lots of time. It did not remove the threat that hung over us. Now our search for a home must be in earnest. We were given the first option to buy the house we were in. We did not feel it was the kind of home we wanted to own, and we felt the price was too high.

The house was not up for sale for more than one week when a man and his wife came to see it. They liked it. They bought it the day after they had been shown through. In a matter of days we were given two months' notice to vacate the premises.

Early in September our second son, Brian, with his wife, Jane, and their two small children came from Calgary to visit with us. We were not the best of hosts. Our hearts were heavy and our necessity was to find a place to move to in a very short time. Brian and Jane were good for our morale, and it was likely a good thing they were there.

We finally found a house not far from where we were living with an asking price of sixty-five thousand dollars. The house was small and consequently all the rooms were small. It was well built and had many excellent features; however, I got the distinct feeling that it was not to be our house. Joy did not agree and wanted to bid on it. She said she could fix it up to be everything we needed. When we came in late in the evening from viewing this house, we talked it over with Brian and Jane, and Joy came to the decision she wanted to bid on the house. Brian sensed that I was disturbed, and when we were alone he said to me, "What do you think about it, Dad?"

I had prayed about this house and felt that I had received a clear answer. To Brian I said, "We have got to bid on it. I feel strongly it would be a mistake for us to buy it. I am convinced that at the last minute our bid will not be accepted. Something is going to stop us from buying that house, but it must not be me."

The four of us sat down in our front room later that evening to discuss the offer we should make. Brian and Jane had just bought a house in Calgary and gave us several useful suggestions.

"What kind of offer do you feel we should make on this house?" My question was directed to Brian. He answered, "I don't think you should bid over sixty thousand."

Jane and Joy both agreed. I called the real estate agent and made an appointment to meet with him the next morning. When I told him our bid he said, "I won't accept a bid like that. It is too low."

"What do you think a fair bid would be?" I asked.

"I don't think the house can be bought for less than sixty-two thousand five hundred," he replied.

"All right, I'll make an offer for that amount, but I want to ask that the stove and fridge and all window drapes and blinds be included in that price."

The interim agreement was drawn up and signed. I wrote out a check for five hundred dollars to seal the bargain, and the real estate man took my offer to present to the owner.

"I'll present this offer at six-thirty this evening. I should have an answer for you by seven o'clock. Will you be at home at that time?"

"Yes, I will, I'll wait for your call. "

All four of us waited for the call that evening. I wondered in my mind whether or not the owner would counteroffer, and if he did, what would we do?

The call was one half hour late in coming. When the phone rang I answered.

"I'm afraid I have some bad news for you," the real estate man said. "Your offer was not accepted. A second offer that came in for sixty-five thousand dollars was accepted. I'm sorry."

"Thank you very much," I said and turned and gave the news to the other three. Brian was the only one who spoke. He said, "That's incredible. He really can't do that, you know. He has to make you a counteroffer."

The next day I phoned another real estate office and made appointments to see two houses in the evening. Right after work Joy and I set off again. We were disappointed in both houses. One had been advertised in the low seventies. It was in a good area and we held high hopes it might be for us. We were both disappointed. The house was run-down inside and out. We both estimated it would cost several thousand dollars to make it livable. As we walked away darkness was setting in. We had arranged to have dinner with Brian and Jane and they planned to leave the next day. Joy was heartsick. I could see it clearly. All she said was, "Let's go home."

"No, dear, we are not going home. I want to show you a house I saw advertised in the paper a short time ago. I made a note of it. It is on the north shore. It said the owner is a retired man who is willing to move out immediately after someone buys the house. I think we should go and have a look at it."

The north shore was a long way from where we were, but I felt we had to see a good house this very night. And it was a good house. The owner was not home so we looked around, very briefly peeking over the gate into the backyard at a garden that was beautiful beyond description. It was like a little park with a lovely lily pond and a rock garden like a little mountain behind it. The garden was full of flowers. The house had sliding glass doors onto a balcony with a beautiful view of the Burrard Inlet. It was everything we had ever hoped to have in a home. Our spirits were revived as we returned home—a little late—to have dinner with Brian and Jane.

That evening I called the real estate man and told him we would like to see the inside of the house. He said, "There is an open house on Saturday, but if you like I will make an appointment for you to go through it tomorrow evening." Tomorrow was Friday. We did not want to wait until Saturday and an appointment was made.

On the way to the appointment the next evening, I said to Joy, "I have decided to bid on this house. There is just one problem. They may want one thousand dollars as a down payment on the offer. I checked our bank account today. All we have is five hundred and thirty-seven dollars."

"If they want one thousand dollars, make the check out for that much. We can get the rest of the money tomorrow," Joy said.

We both loved the house. The inside was more than we had anticipated. It was immaculate. A retired couple had lived in it since it was built six and one-half years ago. They had not only taken good care of it but had continued to improve the house inside and out. The owner was at home and we had a long talk with him. He made tea for us and we discovered that we had some mutual friends.

He was asking seventy-nine thousand five hundred dollars for the house. We made an offer that very evening of seventy-seven five. The owner walked to the door with Joy and me and put one arm around each of us and said, "I'm so glad to know that people like you are going to live in our house. I'm sure your offer will be fine."

It had been agreed that they would wait until the open house was over on Saturday before giving us an answer. It seemed like a long wait. When the real estate man called he said the owner wished to split the difference in his asking price and our offer.

I said immediately that we would agree. The real estate man then said, "When do you want to take possession, and how do you wish to pay for the house?"

Without a moment's hesitation, and without any previous thought, I said, "We would like to move in on the fifteenth of October, and we will have all cash by that date."

The day of that conversation was the eleventh of September. It had not yet entered my mind that it would take a major miracle for us to raise seventy-eight thousand dollars in just over one month.

From the telephone I turned to Joy and said, "We have a house, honey." We hugged one another in sheer ecstasy.

When we had made an offer on the first house I had approached a main line mortgage company and had begun an application for a first mortgage. On Monday morning I called again at this office and spoke to the same man. I related to him how we had lost the first house. He said, "That house should have been yours. They were obliged to make you a counteroffer. Tell me the name of the real estate firm and we will cross them from our list. We don't deal with people who work like that."

"I don't want to cause anyone any trouble. Besides he did us a favor in not counteroffering. We have the house we want."

On Friday of that week our application for a first mortgage in the amount of fifty-five thousand dollars was approved. Upon hearing that news our real estate man had both the owner of the house and myself sign a "waiver of conditions contract" and the house was ours—nearly.

We had approached some friends in Calgary, Alberta, from whom we felt sure we could borrow some of the money we needed. I felt sure help would come from this source. We waited and waited. It did not come. I had waited too long; time was running out. We went to our bank and extended an existing loan. Our son in Calgary sent us a few thousand dollars of the amount we needed. It was Wednesday, the eighth of October.

On Thursday morning I approached a company for a second

mortgage. We completed an initial application and they said they would evaluate the house and let me know as soon as possible. I called by telephone on Friday and arranged an appointment for the late afternoon. Joy had a doctor's appointment that same afternoon and we planned to go as quickly as possible from the doctor's office to the mortgage company. They understood our circumstances and were most obliging and said they would wait for us even if we were a little late.

We were late. We hurried but it was nearly 5:00 P.M. when we reached the mortgage company office. One man, a man we had never seen before, and one secretary waited behind to greet us. At five-thirty all the papers were completed and signed. I said to the man, "We have to have this money by next Tuesday. Wednesday would be all right, but that is the day we are supposed to take possession of the house. Do you think you can have the money for us by Tuesday?"

Please note, it was after business hours on Friday; Monday was Thanksgiving Day and a holiday. Tuesday was the next working day. The man looked at me and said, "It is a miracle you have got this far so quickly. It will take an ongoing miracle to have the money for you by Tuesday. But we will try."

I smiled at his choice of words and wondered if he had any idea what he had just said. "It will take an ongoing miracle to have the money for you by Tuesday."

Shortly after nine o'clock on Tuesday morning the man called my office. He said, "I have a check for you for the full amount of your second mortgage. I'm very sorry but I have no way of getting this check into the hands of your lawyer today. Can you arrange to pick it up?"

"I certainly can," I replied, at the same time as I was saying a prayer of thanks to God for "the ongoing miracle" that had just been fulfilled. "I will pick it up at noon and deliver it to our lawyer myself. Thank you so much for your kindness and your efficiency."

The real estate man had said to me, "When do you want to

take possession, and how do you wish to pay for the house?"

I had answered, "We would like to move in on the fifteenth of October, and we will have all cash by that date."

We were one day ahead of schedule. However, there was a delay of one day. The lawyer for the first mortgage company wished to add a rider in the light of the second mortgage. On Wednesday, the fifteenth, we went over to the house. The original owner had vacated, but we had a key and could let ourselves in. We stood in the living room looking out over the north arm of the Burrard Inlet. It was beautiful. We walked through the sliding glass doors and stood on the balcony. Joy stood by my side and said, "Do you remember a few years ago when you said to me, 'Honey, you will have your house one day with sliding glass doors and a balcony looking out over the ocean?' "

I vaguely remembered. It had been my feeling that this house one day would be ours. I could not specifically remember saying that to Joy. Joy continued, "I never thought that day would come." She put her arm through mine and continued, "Your predictions do come true, darling."

My predictions! Not really. It was all just a part of the most amazing "ongoing miracle" and a part of what can happen when you walk and talk with angels.

XIX

THE CALL

There was never any doubt in my mind that God through His angels had provided for Joy and myself the house on Alberta Street, and then in the fulness of His time had brought us to the house that is now our home. It was a miracle that enabled us to gather together eighty thousand dollars to take possession of this house. Getting that amount of money was one thing; most of it was borrowed and the monthly payments were high. It would take all of my salary to meet these payments. When friends congratulated us on owning our own home, we would say, "Last year we rented a house; this year we are renting money."

Joy and I both gave a great deal of thought to the fact that we might not be able to meet these payments. We did. We believed that God, Who had led us in these strange paths, and Who had looked after us so well, would continue to do so. He did.

We said to ourselves, "If we can just get through the first seven or eight months, we will be all right."

Once again we could have no idea of all that lay ahead.

In the month of September, before we left our rented house on Alberta Street, we decided to have some of the people Joy worked with in for dinner. We had been to their homes and wanted to have them come to ours. At this time the Windmill group was just completing the opening of their fifteenth store. They had expanded from three stores to fifteen in just one year. During the evening the vice-president of the group found an opportunity to speak to me in private. He said, "What do you see ahead for the Windmill?"

He was one of the original owners of the stores but now had become one of a group of businessmen who had taken over and had expanded the stores. I had not given any thought to the future of the company. It looked very secure. However, when I spoke these were the words that came out, "The Windmill has a little less than two years to function under the present management."

No more was said; however, I pondered these words in my mind for some time. I knew where they had come from. My angels had spoken them through my voice. This happened and does happen quite often. It is one form of speaking in tongues. It just happens that the tongue the angels of God use in these instances is our own native tongue and clearly understandable. The vice-president made no further comment.

Some time later I told Joy of this conversation. She listened but made no reply. It was not until very recently that Joy said, "I couldn't see anyway that it would happen" (i.e., that the Windmill would fail).

It did happen and for once right on the time frame that had been given, that is, just under the two years.

Before it happened Joy and I were talking one evening about our future and our individual futures, and I said to her, "You're going to leave the Windmill before another year is over."

Again Joy did not reply, and, again, it was not until very recently that she said to me, "I didn't think there was any possible chance that I would leave the Windmill." But she did. On the ninth of July in 1976 Joy told them at the Windmill that she was leaving for a two-week holiday and that she would not be back. They did not believe her. But she did not return. In the interval many things were to happen.

First, Joy's salary continued to rise. Here again we saw one of the revelations coming true. I had been shown that in the interlude while I was without a church, Joy would come to my aid. At the time we could never have dreamed how long the interval would last. It was now well over a year and we would learn there were many months to go. Joy's rising income permitted us to meet all our payments and care for all our needs. This was only one way in which Joy came to my aid.

One further event that occurred was that Joy, along with two other executive members of the Windmill, went to the United States and Europe for a tour of toy fairs that took her to Chicago; London, England; Nuremberg, Germany; Paris, France; Montreal; New York and then home. Joy was gone for just over five weeks. As her stay in each place was not long and the exact schedule not certain I could not write to her. She phoned often and wrote from every stopping point.

During her absence I wrote the first eighteen chapters of this book. At the time I did not place any significance to the fact that the point at which I ceased writing was at the end of the chapter before this one, entitled "The Call." I did not consciously plan to stop there. It just happened. Nor have I changed the listing of the chapters that I planned to write. They are under the same title and in the same order as first outlined. Of course when I began writing no call had come and no call was anywhere in sight. I had not ceased to believe that the call would come.

In one of the revelations I had been shown quite clearly that God had another church for me, and I had been shown many things about this church. I have now seen most of these things in real life.

After resigning at Gaetz Memorial United Church I had told Joy that a call would come for us before the end of April. I was wrong. It did not come. I said, "Don't worry, it will come this fall."

It didn't. I then said it will come next spring, then next fall. It was painful for both of us, but I was at least learning not to read anything into what God shows us, but to be sure of only what God shows us. At no time was I shown or told when the call would come.

When we were finally settled in our new house and faced with the high monthly payments, I thought it might be possible to find some weekend supply in a church in Vancouver. I felt this might be helpful in many ways. I made some inquiries about nearby churches that might need pulpit supply. Before I had found an opportunity to approach any of the churches mentioned to me, I was shown in a revelation that I would not be permitted to supply any church.

This did not stop me from approaching the churches which were looking for a minister. Among them was Collingwood United Church in South Vancouver. At that time I did not have any idea where it was located. In each case I looked for the phone number of the clerk of session of the church and called. In each case I found that all arrangements for supply were taken care of. This was the only contact I had made with Collingwood United. Now I took the revelation at face value and did not again approach any church.

On a Thursday evening in mid March 1976 the phone rang. It was the chairman of the pastoral relations committee at Collingwood United Church. It was a Mrs. Jean Ashworth, a lady who had been a member of the congregation to which I had ministered in Claresholm, Alberta. We had a delightful conversation. She asked me if I would be interested in being the minister at Collingwood. I assured her I would. She then invited me to meet with the pastoral relations committee at seven-thirty the following Monday evening. I said I would and I did.

I met with the committee for one and one-half hours. They were delightful people and I felt very kindred to them. They asked many questions. I felt they were all excellent questions, and I answered each one as directly, as simply and as honestly as I could. I did not try to impress them in any way. At the end of the one and one-half hour session they thanked me for coming and said they would like to continue their meeting, and they would not take up anymore of my time. They were most congenial and each one rose to shake my hand as I prepared to leave.

"How were the committee members?" Joy asked as I entered our home.

"They were delightful people, dear. I liked them. They are a very humble and sincere group. You know, they didn't ask one smart-aleck question. I really liked them."

I don't think I was in the house for a full ten minutes when the phone rang. It was Jean Ashworth. She said, "The pastoral relations committee would like to recommend to the congregation that we extend a call to you to be our next minister. Will you accept the call?"

"Yes, I will," I replied.

"You will?" There appeared to me to be a note of surprise in her voice.

"Yes, I will, and will you please express my thanks to each member of the committee?"

"Not at all, we thank you."

For the better part of two years there was a closed door and closed so tightly that it seemed as if it would never open. Now, in a matter of a few days, the call had come. Never before had I waited so long for a call. Never before had a call come with such suddenness.

Joy and I had been through such a grueling ordeal that there was a sort of numbness in our system. We were both delighted. It was a quiet delight, not the ecstatic joy that we had known on other such occasions. The numbness would not be removed for a few more months.

It was not long after that night that Joy discovered that the orders she was filling out and placing on the desk of the company president were not being filled. Gradually she learned that the company was in financial difficulty. By the end of May their supply of funds had run out, and by mid June it was evident that the company would soon be forced to declare bankruptcy. By the end of June the company was in receivership and on the ninth of July Joy left her office by careful decision having decided never to return.

My call to Collingwood came through and received the approval of all church courts and was effective the first of July 1976. On Saturday, the third of July, I performed my first wedding and on Sunday, the Fourth of July, conducted services of worship.

It was good to be home. Many letters and phone calls came to us from our friends in Alberta and in Ottawa too.

With the loss of Joy's income we thought we might now have some difficulty. We took stock and thought we might just manage. Then, as before, a check came from an entirely unsuspected source and our needs were met once again.

Joy and I discussed some of the courses that were open to her at this time, and after some minor consultation with the family Joy made the decision to go into business for herself supplying merchandise in the early education field. We chose a name for the company, "Joy's Play and Learn." We registered the company with the provincial government in Victoria. We chose for our emblem a seal with a ball balanced on its nose. Our son Brian once more came to our rescue and assisted us with capital funds. We managed to gather together some merchandise and had made contact with suppliers. We were ready to go.

Then the phone rang and Joy received a most interesting offer. A group of businessmen had purchased four of the former Windmill stores, three in Vancouver and one in Victoria, and had called Joy to ask if she would become the general manager. Her duties would include hiring of all personnel and doing all buying. After consultation and deliberation Joy accepted this position. She began work in this new capacity on the first Monday in August. She had been unemployed for three weeks.

XX

THE END
OF THE IN-BETWEEN

On a lovely evening in late July, before Joy had started her work with the new owners of the four Windmill stores, we were sitting on our patio overlooking the Burrard Inlet. We were both rather quiet in a reflective way. Joy said, "It is nice to be settled again."

She had made the decision to accept this new job offer and at the time felt settled. I said, "We won't be settled until September."

It was true. During the first two weeks of her work Joy found a great deal of turmoil and at one point began making arrangements to go ahead with her own business.

Our conversation on the patio did not end with my remark about September. Joy replied, "Well, this time I hope it lasts."

"Not really, dear; you are only going to be with this company for a short time."

"Don't tell me that," Joy said, with a slight note of alarm in her voice.

"Well, dear, I think you will find that God has some other plans for you, and I think you will see that you will know more about these in about another year."

August came and brought its turbulence, especially for Joy. September followed and with it came a new measure of peace. Both Joy and I were very much aware of the new and beautiful peace that was settling over us and in our lives—our lives individually and our lives together.

September by now had become a month with special significance for us. Two years ago in September we had moved into our house on Alberta Street. In fact, we had moved in on Joy's birthday, the eighteenth of September. One year ago in September we had bought the home we were now living in. Sensing a new significance to this September I felt I wanted to make Joy's birthday something special. I did not express these thoughts to anyone but went quietly about the business of finding a special gift and a special card. September had its own surprises for us.

Shortly after we had arrived in Vancouver our fourth child, a son, John, who had stayed behind in Red Deer, told us that he was planning to buy a piece of property and build a duplex unit to sell as an investment venture. Joy asked if we could put some money into the scheme. We still had our two thousand dollars in bonds. Between Joy and John it was agreed, and we cashed the bonds and gave John both the principal and the interest. John at this time was twenty-one years of age.

This is not really a fair introduction to our son John nor to his activity. When this adventure began he was working with a real estate company and going to the university. That fall he decided to run for a position as an alderman on the Red Deer city council. Many told him he was too young and had no chance of being elected. John did not agree on either count. He ran and he was elected. He bought the land and built the houses. In the summer of 1976 he sold them. We had left everything to John, and although he had shown us the houses we took no part in their erection or sale.

On Friday, the seventeenth of September, a registered letter came to our house from John. It contained a check that represented the total profit from the sale of the duplex. The letter that was also enclosed said "This is a gift for you and Mom, Dad. I wish it could have been more."

It was a sizable check sent with great love. It was big enough to pay off a bank note that we had incurred shortly after arriving in Vancouver and which we had extended to raise money when we bought our house. The note was paid off on Saturday, the eighteenth of September, Joy's birthday. It lifted a great load from our lives and our income.

Through the long months of the "in-between years" the members of our family have been wonderful. They have remained fiercely loyal to both "Mom and Dad"; they have expressed their love in many ways; not once have they lost faith in us, and they have let not only us, but all concerned, know this.

On the same Friday that John's letter arrived, we received a special delivery letter from our youngest son, David; Margaret and Doug had prepared their own celebration for us; we received telephone calls from our two sons in Calgary and their families.

For our own celebration we had made reservations at a delightful spot to have dinner with just the two of us. As we prepared to go out Joy put her arms around me and said, "This year we really have something to celebrate."

We had, indeed, a great deal.

We had a beautiful evening. It was full of peace, joy, laughter and love. Amidst it all there were quiet moments: in one of these, Joy said, "We have certainly been looked after in every way through these difficult years. There is no doubt that God planned all this. But it was not always easy to cling to this faith, was it?"

"No, dear, it wasn't."

Suddenly the numbness was gone. A beautiful elation had returned. The in-between time was over.

It sure was good to be home.

XXI

ANGELS AND
THE SCRIPTURES

The Bible, from beginning to end, is filled with accounts of the angels of God ministering to human beings, in a great variety of ways, and under a multitude of different circumstances. The Bible makes it clear that there is a "ministry of angels." This fact is supported by the life and teaching of Jesus. In the New Testament there is abundant evidence that the disciples and the apostles were well aware of the presence and the activities of God's angels. In this chapter we shall turn to the Scriptures for just a few examples of the presence of angels in the affairs of mankind.

In one of the familiar Old Testament stories, the story known to many of us as "Jacob's Ladder," the angels of God encounter Jacob as he is journeying from his own home to the land of his mother's brother. Actually, Jacob was fleeing the wrath of his brother, Esau. As Jacob tarried for the night and lay down to sleep, he was engaged in conversation with one or more of God's angels. Jacob was given information as to the direction his life would take from that day on. You may read of this encounter in Genesis, chapter twenty-eight. In case you think that this was merely a dream and nothing more, hear from the lips of Jacob his own assessment of this meeting and all that happened afterwards. In Genesis, chapter forty-eight, we meet Jacob as an old man. He is about to bless his son, Joseph. In verses fifteen and sixteen we read:

And he [Jacob] blessed Joseph, and said, "The God before whom my fathers Abraham and Isaac walked, the God who has led me all my life long to this day, THE ANGEL WHO HAS REDEEMED ME FROM ALL EVIL, bless the lads . . ."

Jacob's life was changed by the first encounter with angels. Jacob acknowledged this in his reference to "the angel who has redeemed me from all evil." This assertion also gives evidence of awareness of the presence of angels in his life.

There is another equally famous story in the Old Testament known to us as "Moses and the Burning Bush." The attention of Moses is caught by a bush that appears to be burning and yet is not consumed by the fire. He turns aside to see this wondrous sight, and from the bush an angel of God speaks to Moses. This significant day in the life of Moses is recorded for us in the Book of Exodus, chapter three, verses two to twelve. I quote just briefly from verse two: "And the angel of the Lord appeared to him [Moses] in a flame of fire out of the midst of a bush. . . ."

This story is well worth reading again. It is delightful. Moses is next engaged in conversation by God, Who tells him what He wants him to do. Moses is not certain that he can do it, and above all else he is not sure that anyone will believe him when he tells them that an angel has appeared unto him and God has spoken to him. It is indeed easy to understand how Moses felt.

In Psalm ninety-one, verses eleven and twelve, in the King James Version, we read these beautiful words of God's truth:

> For he shall give his angels charge over thee, to keep thee in all thy ways. They shall bear thee up in their hands lest thou dash thy foot against a stone.

In the New English Bible these words are translated in this manner: "For he [God] has charged his angels to guard you wherever you go, to lift you on their hands. . . ."

Both translations keep faith with the action and intent of God who communicated this beautiful truth to the psalmist, whoever he was, through an angel who was present with the psalmist not only at that time but in all likelihood throughout his whole life.

There are even more instances of the presence and activity of angels recorded for us in the New Testament. These stories are beautiful. In our modern world we are surrounded by man's accomplishments in science and technology, and we have almost lost the importance, the beauty, the truth and the significance of the ministry of angels which still goes on. We shall mention only a few of these accounts.

In the Book of Acts, chapter twelve, Herod the King "laid violent hands on some who belonged to the Church. He killed James . . . with the sword . . . he proceeded to arrest Peter also."

Peter was kept in prison and heavily guarded. It was Herod's intention to have Peter publicly executed after the feast of unleavened bread. In verse seven we read that on the very night when Herod was about to bring Peter out ". . . an angel of the Lord appeared . . ." and Peter was rescued. There is, however, an even deeper significance to this story. We find it in four little words recorded in Acts, chapter twelve, verse fifteen. At the same time that Peter was sleeping in his cell on that fateful night, there were gathered together many of the faithful members of the new church. They had gathered by arrangement at the home of Mary, the Mother of John Mark, the author of the Gospel According to St. Mark. When Peter was released from his cell by an angel, the angel escorted Peter into a dark street and then departed, leaving him standing there. Peter decided to go to the home of Mary, where he knew his friends had gathered and were praying for him.

When his knocking on the outer door was finally heard, "a maid named Rhoda" came to see who it was. Rhoda was so overwhelmed with joy at the sound of Peter's voice that she ran back to tell the others that Peter was at the gate. It seemed too good to be true; they could not believe it. They said, "It is his angel." (Acts 12:15, KJV)

Almost all translations of the Bible use this exact wording. However, in the New English Bible, the verse is translated, "It must be his guardian angel."

From this and many other passages of Scripture in the New Testament, it is clear that the followers of Jesus were well acquainted with God's ministry of angels. They knew from first-hand experience that the angels of God were engaged with them in their ministry. They were rescued by God's angels many times. Their lives were saved by angels more than once. The angels spoke to them giving them direction and on more than one occasion telling them of things that were yet to come.

One more example of these facts is recorded for us in the twenty-seventh chapter of the Book of Acts. This time it was the Apostle Paul who had and recorded an experience with one of God's angels. Paul was journeying by ship along the shores of Crete. It was late in the season; winter was coming. Paul felt the captain should not try to proceed on the journey but winter at a port where they had taken temporary refuge. Neither the captain nor the crew agreed with Paul, and they cast off when a favorable wind came along. The weather soon changed and a winter storm swept down upon them. The ship and the crew were no match for the fierce gale. This part of the story is recorded in verses ten to twenty. The part to which I wish to specifically refer you is found in verses twenty-one to twenty-six. Here we will record only the salient parts of these verses:

> . . . Paul came forward and said, "Men, you should have listened to me . . . however, I beg you to keep up your spirits for no one's life is going to be lost, though we shall lose the ship. I know this because last night, the angel of God to whom I belong, and whom I serve, stood by me and said, 'Have no fear, Paul! You must stand before Caesar. And God, as a mark of his favor towards you, has granted you the lives of those who are sailing with you.' I am certain that everything will happen exactly as I have been told . . ."

I have quoted from *The New Testament in Modern English*, by J. B. Phillips. However, it does not matter from what translation you read this experience; the conversation between Paul and "an angel of the God whom I serve" is almost identical. Certainly every translation keeps faith with the story as reported in the King James Version of the Holy Bible.

I wish to turn now to Jesus. Jesus told the parable of the rich man and a poor man named Lazarus. The parable is recorded in the Gospel According to St. Luke in chapter sixteen, verses nineteen to thirty-one. The particular verse I wish to call to your attention is twenty-two. Jesus is speaking and he says, "The poor man died and was carried by the angels to Abraham's bosom [i.e., to heaven]."

In many ways and in many places Jesus made reference to God's ministry with angels.

There is one more New Testament reference to angels that I wish to note and quote. It is recorded in John Mark's Gospel in chapter one, verse thirteen: "And he [Jesus] was in the wilderness forty days . . . and the angels ministered to him."

Please note that the word "angel" here is pluralized. A number of angels ministered to Jesus not only during his days in the wilderness but all through his ministry. It was by the support of unseen angels that Jesus walked over the surface of a body of water.

This is not an adequate treatment of the theme of the activity of angels in the Bible. Nor is it meant to be. It is, however, a brief presentation of the truth that runs like a golden chord throughout the Bible, this truth that the angels of God have always participated in the affairs of men. There is a ministry of angels. In the Bible angels walked and talked with men and women. There was a ministry of angels in biblical days; there is a ministry of angels in the world today. The ministry of angels functions entirely according to the will of God. For many centuries not much mention was made concerning the ministry of angels. In our present age this ministry is being revealed to many in a new and exciting way. I am only one who, in the fullness of God's time and for God's reasons, has been called by God "to walk and talk with angels."

XXII

ANGELS
AND YOU

There is one more passage of Scripture to which careful consideration should be given by those who seek to understand the ministry of angels. It is found in the eighteenth chapter of the Gospel of St. Matthew. This passage really should have been included in the previous chapter. I purposely left it until now for it speaks regarding "angels and you."

In this Scripture Jesus is speaking. As the chapter begins, the disciples come to Jesus and ask, "Master, who is the greatest in the kingdom of heaven?"

In answer Jesus first places a child in their midst and says, "Truly, I say to you, unless you turn and become like children you will never enter the kingdom of heaven."

Further along in this chapter, verse ten, Jesus speaks the following interesting words:

175

See that you do not despise one of these little ones; for I tell you that in heaven their angels always behold the face of my Father who is in heaven.

This quotation is from the Revised Standard Version. The King James Version is identical except for the use of "ye" rather than "you." These words are of such importance that we should examine them from as many translations as possible.

First, from the New English Bible:

Never despise one of these little ones; I tell you, they have guardian angels in heaven who look continually on the face of my heavenly Father.

The New Testament in Modern English, by J. B. Phillips, gives us this translation:

Be careful that you never despise a single one of these little ones—for I tell you that they have angels who see my Father's face continually in heaven.

The issue that is raised here, and well worth consideration, is this, "Does every single human being have an angel of God assigned to him or her?"

Of little children, Jesus said, ". . . their angels do always behold the face of my Father. . . ." Note the plural, "their angels."

We then are on very safe ground when we infer that every child born into this life on earth has been assigned by God an angel to be with him or her. My angels confirm that this is so. An angel of God is present at every birth and walks with every child.

Many questions now come flooding into the mind. What is the purpose of the angel? Does he or she stay with every human being all through life? Are all angels alike? Do they all have the same purpose?

The questions most often asked of me are different still. I am asked, "What is an angel? What do they look like? Have you seen one?"

The first purpose for which God assigns angels to every human being is this: they are to guard the human life to which they are assigned from all forces, including evil, other than the forces of God. There are many factors and forces in existence that cannot be seen by the human eye or detected by any of the purely human sensory organs. Some of these forces work against individual human beings. The angels of God are charged to protect us against these forces with which we are unable to deal directly.

This is not the only purpose of angels. However, just as God does not require the same actions and reactions from every human being, so also God does not give the same purpose to every angel that walks with a human being. Let us note that the expression "walk with a human being" is merely a method of expressing the presence of an angel with some person on earth. The angels are able to participate in life in heaven and life on earth at the same time. They are able to move great distances in the flash of a moment. They are not "locked in" to time and space as we humans are. Time is quite different in eternity, and it is very clear that in some way the future is already known to God and much of it is known to His angels.

The angels do not all have the same rank and all are not permitted to use the great powers that are in existence in the universe to the same extent. That is, some angels have greater authority and are accorded greater freedom in the use of these powers.

Do the angels stay with everyone all through a lifetime on earth? Not necessarily. When a person, by deliberate choice, sets out to live apart from God and God's purpose, the angels of

God can and may begin to withdraw from that person. My angels tell me that in some cases the withdrawal is complete. One more thing is certain: just as there is an angel present at every birth, so also there is an angel present at every death. At the death of our human body, an angel is present to transport us or escort us to the place prepared for us in God's eternal kingdom. As we are looking only at the presence and purpose of angels in human affairs, there is no intent to deal here with the subject of death and life in eternity in any depth or completeness. It is my belief that the next realm of life does not take place in one large expanse of the same place. Jesus said, "In my Father's house are many rooms." I believe that human beings use their life on earth in a wide diversity of fashions and with many different goals. Therefore, we human beings end our life on earth and enter God's eternity at wide and divergent levels of spiritual development. It is my belief, therefore, that we are taken to many different places to continue our spiritual growth. This thought frightens some people; they fear they will be separated from their loved ones. Not necessarily so. In a family on earth it is common for all members to live in one house and yet be at many levels of growth and development. Little children stay at home all week; older children go to school and some perhaps to universities. Other adult members of the family go out to work and some travel great distances to pursue their employment. All are at the same time together and yet "in different places." So it will be for some in eternity; we may well continue to live together in a bond of love and yet go to many different places as we seek to grow and mature in our spiritual pilgrimage of life . . . that only begins on earth.

What is an angel? Let us say what surely we must understand—that in any area of knowledge, including knowledge about God's angels, we can only know a very small portion of what God knows. No one on earth, no one, has complete knowledge or understanding of all of God or all of God's activities or even of any one segment of knowledge. We do not know much about angels or much about what they do. We do, however, have insight into their activities. An angel, first of all, is a servant of God living in God's eternity. Some angels are trained and sent to walk and work with specific people on earth. These angels have access to life in eternity and life on earth at the same time. That is, they move easily and freely on the earthly plane of life and in the heavenly plane of life.

Angels have a great desire, and have developed a tremendous capacity, to love God and to share love with God. The great aim of their life is to serve God, to obey God and to cooperate with God in His work. In one word, God's work is "people," people on earth and people in eternity. Thus, in serving God the angels serve people. Many people on earth who have found great satisfaction and fulfillment in serving God and in seeking to know Him thus have caught a glimpse of the great awe, reverence and adoration with which angels approach and worship God. Thus many on earth have a foretaste of what it means "to enjoy God forever."

All angels are not engaged with human life on earth. We can only catch brief glimpses of what the next realms of life will be like, and we can know only limited amounts concerning the activities of heaven. It is important to note that we do have glimpses of insight. We are never left entirely to our own limitations or our own resources.

What do angels look like? They may take on more than one form. In some respects they can be surprisingly like we human beings. In fact, angels sometimes take on a complete human form and appear to people on earth. The Bible speaks of the need to be kind to strangers who come to our home and cautions us "that we might be entertaining angels unawares." The specific reference is in the Book of Hebrews, chapter thirteen, verse two, and says, "Be not forgetful to entertain strangers: for thereby some have entertained angels unawares."

Mostly angels appear in a spiritual body that cannot be seen by our physical sight. However, many people about to depart this earth in what we have so fallaciously labeled "death" have already received some part of their spiritual sight and have seen angels in their presence.

Recently I flew into the airport at Calgary, Alberta. I was met at the airport by our son David and our friend Bob Millar. While we waited for my luggage to come off the plane, a young man, a former member of my congregation in Red Deer, approached and wished to speak to me. He told me about his mother's death. She had been an invalid for many years and I had ministered to her. She was a true child of God. On the evening of her death, her son was standing at the foot of her hospital bed. She asked him to move, for she said, "You are standing in front of that gentleman."

Her son turned but saw no one. Thus he faced his mother again, resuming his same position at the foot of the bed. His mother now spoke with just a bit more insistence in her voice; she said, "Son, please don't stand in front of that visitor with your back to him."

To please his mother, he moved. He could not get this incident off his mind and sought me out to talk about it. In his own mind he thought this presence might have been an angel. He wanted confirmation.

"Yes, T., it was an angel sent by God to be with your mother at that time and to escort her into eternity. Your mother was already beginning to live in her spiritual body, and, therefore, she had spiritual sight and could see what you could not."

It appears that this angel looked very much like a man, and yet there was some distinction about him—enough to have the lady refer specifically to him as a "gentleman." Many people have told me of personal experiences they have had with an angel, and in almost every case there was something that set apart the angel and made it possible to know it was an angel.

The Bible is filled with instances where angels appear to people on earth in a garment of blinding light. Some who tell me that they have seen an angel say that the light was so blinding they could not see beyond the great light. This is a highly developed spiritual form. It is the form in which Christ appeared to the Apostle Paul on the Damascus road. Paul was blinded by the dazzling light. It was many days before his sight was restored through a spiritual healing.

We have mentioned three forms in which angels may appear. Undoubtedly there are more. Whether or not any angel has wings, as we sometimes see them depicted in books, I do not know. I doubt it. My angels do not and anyone who has told me they have seen an angel say they do not have wings. It may be that this is simply an attempt to portray the great speeds with which angels are able to move.

Angels and you! Whoever you are, dear reader, the likelihood is great that as you read these lines an angel of God is looking over your shoulder. Perhaps your angel nudged you into buying this book.

Many people ask, "Will I be able to talk with my angel?" Some of you will, not all. The decision is neither mine nor yours. It is God's. Some people have no desire to communicate with an angel. If your desire is great, then ask God in prayer and be patient. In days to come more and more people will communicate with angels sent by God.

XXIII

GOD
IN THE
WORLD
TODAY

Of God in the world of His day, Jesus said, "My Father worketh hitherto, and I work" (John 5:17). The modern translators put this identical message into the language of our day in this fashion, "My Father is working still, and I work."

There is no reason to believe that God has ever stopped working in His world. There is, in fact, a great deal of evidence to support the idea that God is very much at work in His world today.

Our first premise then is this: the world, in fact, the universe belongs to God and God is at work in the world. So is Jesus Christ and so also is the Holy Spirit. There is also a ministry of angels at work in the world.

We might well ask, "Why then is the world in the throes of so much anguish, so much confrontation, so much distrust, so much selfishness, so much hatred?"

The answer to a very large degree lies in the fact that God gave to man—men and women—a free will. He permits us to make our own choices. God never takes from us our free will. The angels who walk with us cannot take from us our free will. Mostly our choices are made in self-interest, and all too often they are made in utter selfishness. This is not only so of individuals but also of nations and leagues of nations. In Jesus Christ, God was showing man how he wanted man to live. Jesus gave us all the moral laws we need to live a beautiful life. They are set out for us in the New Testament and are easy to read and understand. By their own choices, more people than not have rejected this way of living. It is our own choices, more than any other factor, that have brought us into the chaos in which we live. Man, by his rejection of God, in whatever form this rejection may take, lives as if he owned the earth.

There are, of course, other factors. There are evil forces at work in the world. These forces are able to command the co-operation of some human beings. These forces need not be a cause of fear or alarm to those who by their own choice align their lives with God in daily trust for His protection. In His model prayer, the Lord's Prayer, Jesus tells us to ask God daily, ". . . lead us not into temptation . . . deliver us from evil. . . ."

I believe a good translation of these words is, ". . . strengthen us in every temptation . . . protect us, or keep us safe, against every evil. . . ."

For all those who live in complete trust of God, one of the tasks of the angels is to strengthen us in temptation and protect us against evil, particularly the evil that we cannot see and therefore cannot deal with. If we deliberately choose evil, knowing what we are doing, the angels may not protect us against it, unless within our wills we really wish to resist evil and for a moment are acting in a manner not consistent with our own real will.

There can be no doubt that evil forces within the universe are having a great deal of success in our age.

Let us come to the heart of the theme for this chapter, "God in the World Today." What is God doing in the world today? Or, if you prefer, "What in the world is God doing!"

It should not be necessary but is perhaps prudent to begin by acknowledging that no human being can know all that God is doing on earth. There is a greater gap between the mind of God and mind of any one of us than there is between an atomic scientist and his two-year-old child. The two-year-old knows the father, loves the father, trusts the father and understands to a great extent that the father goes to work, protects the family and along with mother provides for food and cares for the family.

If our minds could comprehend all of God, then it is clearly evident that God would be too small for the universe. In fact, this is one of man's great perils—we continue to create in our own minds a God that is too small for life in a complex atomic-energy age. One way in which we reduce God to our own size is by demanding to know "all about God" or all that God knows.

Nevertheless, God has seen to it that we can know Him, can receive and return His love, can know some of the things He is doing, and we can cooperate with Him in some of the things He is doing. Then, first of all, God is at work in the world by working in individual lives. Second, God is at work in the world working through individual lives. Thirdly, God is at work in the world through His ministry of angels and through the work of the Holy Spirit.

God is not only at work in the world through individuals, he is also at work through His church, through groups of people outside the church, and through such groups as the ministry of healing that goes on through doctors, nurses, hospitals. God is also at work in nations partly through individuals but also more directly than we could ever imagine. And He is at work between nations.

God is at work in the world in other ways. For instance, there is the great redemptive ministry of Jesus Christ, the son of God. Jesus too, of course, is at work in and through individuals and the church and in many other ways. For the Christian, the redeeming love of God comes to us through Christ, and our faith in God is centered in Christ. For that great mass of humanity that does not have Jesus at the center of its religion, God has other ways of bringing them to fulfillment in this life and into His eternal kingdom in the next plane of life. The angels that work with us represent not only God, but also Christ and also the Holy Spirit. They are ministering angels on behalf of all three. These angels minister to the people who do not place Christ at the center of their religion, as well as with those who do. Thus Christ the Savior is at work in every human life.

I have heard some people express the thought that there would be no Jews in heaven for they do not acknowledge Jesus as their Savior. It is amazing how we can overlook some parts of the Scriptures. On the Mount of Transfiguration, where Jesus had taken Peter and James and John, Jesus first takes on the appearance of glory. This beautiful and significant event is recorded for us in the Gospel According to St. Luke, chapter nine, verses twenty-eight to thirty-six. The account of the event is virtually the same in every translation. For easier understanding, I will quote from a modern translation, *The New Testament in Modern English,* by J. B. Phillips:

> And then, while he [Jesus] was praying, the whole appearance of his face changed and his clothes became white and dazzling. And two men were talking with Jesus. They were Moses and Elijah . . . revealed in heavenly splendor, and their talk was about the way he [Jesus] must take and the end he must fulfill in Jerusalem (Luke 9:29-31).

The point is, two men, Moses and Elijah, both Jews, both very much alive, both now residing in heaven, came to earth for a brief meeting with Jesus. These two men could not have had a higher responsibility than this one assigned to them by God, to work with Jesus and to bring this message to Jesus from God. Actually, what they brought to Jesus here was an answer to his prayer for confirmation by God that he was on the right path in going to Jerusalem and facing and accepting crucifixion. This was only one method of confirmation that Jesus sought to the hard truth that God really wanted him to die on a cross.

God is at work in the whole world and with all people; for all people are God's people.

On the Mount of Transfiguration, we have been introduced to still another aspect of God's ministry of angels. Most of us will receive protection and guidance through the angel, or angels, that God has assigned to walk with us through life. God does, however, have countless numbers of angels having differing skills and specialties. God can and does send additional angels to the assistance of mankind in times of special peril or special need. Your angel may receive help from other angels, often specialized angels, on occasions when there is a demand for such intervention.

God is at work in the world today in many other ways. God is still calling people into His work. He is still calling individuals for special assignments in the world today, and He is still choosing groups of people for special tasks. When He calls an individual or a group, He then puts them through a preparation period and guides them into the place where their task is to be performed. After God has called someone into His work, the training and the performing of the work may go on at the same time.

In days not too long gone, ministers, priests and rabbis used to speak quite freely about "being called by God into His service." Some fifteen or twenty years ago, when the church fell under great criticism and there began the great falling away of people from the church, many young student ministers began to say that they were not called by God into His service, rather they just chose this way of life as a career. Some ordained ministers, especially among the younger group, joined in the chorus stating that they had not been called. For a few years, some student ministers, as they approached graduation and ordination, stated they would not go into the pastorate but rather would choose careers in the field of social service.

Many ministers, myself included, continued to believe that God called us into His service. I am still of this mind. My call by God into the ministry was clear to me, although at first I found it difficult to believe that God really wanted "me" for a minister. Among my classmates this reluctance was fairly general.

A few years after I was ordained, a young man came to my office and said that he wanted to go into the ministry and that he felt God was calling him, "But," he said, "how can I be sure?"

I recognized the struggle he was having. It was familiar. Among the things I said to him was, "If God in some strange way has laid His hand upon you, you will not escape. He will lead you into the ministry."

Some years later I received a letter from this young man saying, "The hand of God was truly laid upon me, and I did not escape. I am now an ordained minister, and I am beginning a ministry on my first pastoral charge."

His letter was filled with gratitude for our conversation and in it he recalled many things we had shared together.

The truth that in my early life God called me into His ministry has become clearer to me through the years. I now understand the nature of the call and many of the circumstances surrounding it, particularly with regard to the timing. Then, as I have told you, God came into my life in a new way, introducing me to two of His angels, who have walked with me through all of my life and who walk and talk with me today.

A call came to me for a second time. This time the call was in clear, concise English. There was no mistake. This time the call was to a continuation of ministry and also to a new and extended kind of ministry.

Following this second call came a long period of preparation. Some of the conditions of the preparation were not shown to me ahead of time and proved to be tremendously difficult. In fact, for two years my wife and I were led into and through a wilderness.

The relevant point is simply this: God is still calling men and women into His service, into ministries of many different kinds.

God is not only calling and preparing individual men and women for His service in a great new venture, God is choosing, calling and preparing churches and groups of people both within and outside of the church, for work with Him and for Him on earth. One significant part of the preparation of an individual or a church congregation is this: God often leads the person or group into and through a period of weakness and often humiliation. I am convinced that God permitted His whole church to be brought into a time of rejection, a time of great criticism and a time of humiliaton and weakness. In fact, in one of the revelations given to me by the angels of God, I was shown that many churches would be brought low, some very near to the point of death. The same revelation showed that not all churches would be brought low, but that some would be given greater strength than they had had before. The purpose for some churches being strengthened while others were brought low is so that God will always have His witnesses on earth, and the church will not lose the complete confidence of God's people. Still another reason for the strengthening of some congregations is to challenge those brought low to a greater enlightenment, service and ministry.

When God enters this fully into the life of a church or a minister, the resulting confrontation can be grueling and punishing. Punishment is never for the sake of punishment alone; its purpose is to purify and to strengthen. There is one more dimension involved: God is trying to teach the individual, or the group or the church that he cannot function adequately in his own strength. The power of God is needed for adequate performance.

What God is trying to say to His people is this: "I want to use you in a great new ministry; I want to use you in a great new age. The contest will be grueling. Many unseen and unknown forces will try to block your efforts. You can only succeed in My strength. First then, let Me show you how inadequate your own strength is. Now, if you will let Me pour in My power we can do great things together."

God might well be using the churches that are flourishing to say to us, "See, it can be done. You'd better strive to find out how."

There may still be another element in what is happening to the church today. The church has shown itself through history to be hesitant to change. Jesus had more trouble with the priestly class and the church leaders of His day than He had with those outside the church. It may be that God is indicating to the church that if it will not rise to the height and function in His power, then He may have to bypass the church and find alternate methods of bringing in a new age on earth.

There is one more activity of God in the world today that is becoming increasingly clear. God is still bestowing His great gifts upon men and women. It may even be that in the world today God is bestowing His gifts upon more people than at any other time in history. You will find the list of the gifts God set out for us by the Apostle Paul in his First Letter to the Christians in the city of Corinth, that is, in First Corinthians, chapter twelve, verses twenty-seven to thirty-one. The whole of chapter twelve deals with the gifts of God. They are listed for us in this way (King James Version):

And God hath set some in the church, first apostles, secondarily prophets, thirdly teachers, after that miracles, then gifts of healing, helps, governments, diversities of tongues.

J. B. Phillips translates these verses in this manner:

And in His church God has appointed first some to be His messengers, secondly, some to be preachers of power, thirdly, teachers. After them He has appointed workers of spiritual power, men with gifts of healing, helpers, organizers and those with gifts of speaking in tongues.

Phillips translates the word "prophet" as "messenger." I believe this is an excellent translation. If you look up the meaning of the word "prophet" in a reliable dictionary you will find this definition: "a messenger of God." Early in my encounter with two of God's angels one of the angels said to me, "Ed, you are going to be a mesesnger for God; we will give you messages from God and your responsibility will be to deliver them in exactly the form in which you receive them."

They told me a great deal more about the reception and delivery of such mesages, and many times in very special circumstances I have received and delivered messages. Sometimes the message was for a whole congregation and was delivered as a part of or as a whole sermon. On a number of occasions when people have come to me for counseling or help in a crisis situation, I have received and delivered messages to them. Some such people were entirely unknown to me until the moment they entered my office. It is a thrilling experience to receive a message from

God through the ministry of an angel and see a life light up, or come alive or be restored, sometimes from great depths.

God is very much at work in His world, and He is bestowing His gifts upon many.

We have made reference to the fact that God is preparing to enter the world in a new way, that is, to bring one age to an end and begin a new age on earth. One question that has been asked is, "Will this require taking away the free will of man?"

Not at all. Mankind's deep longings are for "peace," "love," "justice," "freedom"—"freedom from tyranny, from disease, from poverty." Our blindness to both the nearness and the goodness of God, together with our own selfishness and in some cases arrogance, causes us to act in a manner that is contrary to our real will. We can say the same thing this way, "we are capable of behavior that is totally opposed to our character." In this we are pushed, or aided and abetted by the forces of evil, or, if you prefer, by the negative forces of and in the world.

In a new age God will become so real to us that his very presence will strengthen us, and in ways we may well not understand, God will lead us into living and loving in complete accord with our real will.

When will this age come? We do not know. In the first chapter of the Book of Acts, beginning at verse four, Jesus tells his disciples to wait in Jerusalem until ". . . the Holy Spirit is fully come upon you." The disciples ask Jesus, "Lord, is this the time when you are going to restore the Kingdom of Israel?" Jesus answers, "You cannot know times and dates which have been fixed by the Father's sole authority. . . ."

One thing I have learned is this: it is impossible to know God's time and God's timing. In some things the angels will give you the exact time. In the great events, God's time is known only to God.

There are many people who believe that God has already begun the preparation for a new day. Whether this day will happen within the lifetime of any of us we cannot know. It is a thrilling time to be alive, especially for God's people. It is a great time to be God's church on earth.

One aspect of the age in which we live and of the age which is to come is this: "More and more people will work in close conjunction with the angels of God."

XXIV

REVELATIONS INTERPRETED

Soon after two of God's angels made their presence in my life known to me, they began to present to me a series of messages from God in an unusual way. I have chosen to call these messages "revelations." Some would call them "visions." Harper's *Bible Dictionary* defines a vision in these words: "a sight presented to the mind," and defines a revelation as "the act of disclosing or communicating the divine to men." I believe that my angels communicated the divine to me. Some of these revelations were interpreted for me at the time they were given: some were partly interpreted, and some were simply presented and left with me. One in particular was not made clear at all until just this week, the last week in October, nineteen hundred and seventy-six.

I wish to share with you now the meaning of some of these revelations, beginning with the one I call "this is it." The revelation began with the phone in our home ringing and my answering it. When I said, "Hello," a voice on the other end said, "This is Dr. Barclay calling. I hear you are going to Vancouver."

I turned to Joy and called out with great glee, "Honey, this is it!"

This revelation came a full two years before we left Gaetz Memorial United Church. It is also important to state that I had been told by my angels in clear English that God had a new task for me and that I would be moved to a new church. Thus, my reception of the vision was blurred by my own expectation.

To the voice that identified itself as "Dr. Barclay," I replied in the affirmative. The voice went on to say, "I plan to be in Vancouver. I will meet you there."

Living in England today, there is a renowned theologian, an ordained minister, who is an acknowledged biblical interpreter. His name is Dr. William Barclay. The intent of this part of the message was that we would move to Vancouver, and there, over a period of time, the revelations would be interpreted by events that would occur, by circumstances in which we would be caught up and by the Holy Spirit. This was not the interpretation that I put upon the message at the time I received it. I expected to be moved to a new church. I did not dream that God would leave us without a church, thus I assumed that we would be moving to Vancouver and going directly to a new church. I was wrong in the timing. We did move to Vancouver. We did eventually take up work in a church in Vancouver. It was the two-year interlude that was not foretold and could not be foreseen. Not only did my own expectation get in the way of the correct reception of this revelation, but so also did my great, exuberant joy. For those who work with God's angels, one part of the training is to prepare you to handle this exultation.

The voice on the telephone continued to speak, but in a manner that was muffled and in a tone that gradually faded away. Again I turned to Joy and said, "I can't understand a single word this man is saying." Then there was a long silence. The silence was broken by a Canadian Broadcasting Corporation radio time signal. The time signal begins with a series of beeps and then a voice says, "At the long dash following the silence, the time will be. . . ."

In Vancouver, this part of the revelation soon became clear. Events were confusing; communication with the angels was first garbled and then faded into a long silence.

The time signal further indicated that "timing" in this revelation would be confusing and would play a major role.

In the revelation, as it was being presented to my mind, after the long silence in the time signal, the voice spoke very clearly once more. It said, "Your stars are high. You will be moved in the fall."

When we were left without a church at the end of June 1974, it was a strange set of circumstances that took us to Vancouver, and an even stranger set of circumstances that kept us there. During the summer, we twice moved out of Vancouver; once to Victoria where Joy had accepted a very good position, and once to Calgary, Alberta, where circumstances had led us. Each time we were brought back to Vancouver by events that were not in any way of our making.

In Vancouver, I fully expected to be moved to a new church "in the fall." The first fall came and went without even a whisper. In the second fall, we were moved to our new home. This was the move foretold in the revelation. I still clung to the belief that a church would come, and we would be back in the full-time ministry. For the members of our family this was a fading hope, and, again, I stood almost entirely alone.

The last part of this revelation indicated that communication would eventually become clear again and following the silence, there would come a new period of time, that is, a new beginning. The silence was long and the confusion great. The silence was finally broken when my angels spoke to me one day as I was driving my car home from work. For a while, communication was off and on. There were times when I was led into the presence of people who were to be ministered to in a variety of ways. Such moments were for me very rewarding, and there were also signs that the day would come when I would be back in the full ministry. I tried very hard to communicate this to the people I loved dearly—my wife and family. They, however, were not experiencing the things I was, and under the circumstances it is easy to see why they could not fully understand or believe. What I was learning was this, "When God wants someone to believe, He will lead them into belief; if God does not want someone to believe, no human effort can make that person or those people believe." When you work with God's angels, total trust in God and total dependence on God for the work He leads you to do are of utmost importance. I was told this from the very beginning. The training through which both Joy and I have been led has made it clear beyond a doubt.

The next revelation that I wish to share with you is the one I call "solitary confinement." I did not receive the interpretation for this revelation until four years after I had received it. The events foretold did not even begin to occur until three and one-half years after the revelation came. The part of the revelation that was clear was that I would be put into a solitary confinement. The confinement the revelation referred to did not occur until late spring in 1976. There was no way this revelation could have been understood or put into the right time frame, except by the meaning being given by God's angels, who are instruments of the Holy Spirit as well as messengers and ministers for God. Thus the meaning came as a surprise to me.

About two years before we left Gaetz Memorial United Church, my angels said to me in clear English, "Ed, we are going to put you in a solitary confinement for a little while."

Their idea of a "little while" and mine are two different things. Four years to me is not a little while. Not out of one short human life. The angels, however, do not measure even human life by the span of years that we spend on earth. Life is eternal and life on earth is just a small span of the life we live that begins on earth but continues in God's eternity. Thus they persist in their statement that four or fourteen years is "a little while."

When this revelation began, it was late one evening. It was dark and I was standing entirely alone. What I know now is that I was at that moment already in isolation. What I also know now is that the date for that day, the day the event of the revelation began, was in the first two weeks of March 1976. In front of me there was a long, sloping hill. This simply meant that for a while life was going to be an uphill pull. To the left of me there was a roadway curving from the bottom of this hill to the top. At the bottom of the hill along the roadway to my left there was a row of houses brightly lighted and signifying great comfort and security. I could not see anyone, but I seemed to have the feeling that Joy was in one of these houses. My desire at the time was to escape the confinement I was in but I wished Joy to come with me. For a long time Joy would not come. Finally she appeared and I took her by the hand and ran up the roadway to the top of the hill where there now appeared a gateway that would lead to freedom. As we approached the gate, a truck appeared and enemy soldiers jumped out and took me, separating me from Joy, and placed me in an even greater solitary confinement.

The experience through which Joy and I had been led was so grueling that we had come to the place where we did not talk about it. I still believed that "someday" I would be back in a church. For Joy and the family, any hope of this was gone. Mostly we just did not talk about it. When the call finally and suddenly came, Joy was delighted for me, but what I did not know was this: the hurt of these events and years was by now so painful for Joy that she weighed heavily the possibility of remaining in her career in the business world and sending me off to the church alone.

Joy's life, like mine, was fully in the hands of God. God had led both of us down some strange and demanding paths. He did not at any time leave us alone. Joy's struggle was her own. God meant it to be so. He kept me right out of the way and right out of the decision making.

The day finally came when Joy arrived home from work and announced, "I have quit my job. I start my two weeks' holiday today and I told them I will not be back."

I make no comparison with any human being and Jesus. However, I have done a great deal of contemplating on the events of these days, and I have thought more than once that God led Jesus out into the wilderness, and there He let Jesus face three great temptations. I believe that God leads His most humble servants out into a wilderness, and some He still faces with temptations to struggle with and decisions to make. It is a most difficult time. The wilderness is tremendously lonely. It is, however, a time of great strengthening.

Joy did not go back to her job. From the moment we started our ministry at Collingwood she has not only been at my side, but she has branched out once more into a ministry of her own. She has already been invited to speak to the men's club. After hearing her, they invited her to come into the pulpit and tell more of her story. Her ministry is not confined to the church, and it has only just begun.

In quite a number of the revelations I would see two churches. I found this very puzzling. I tried to determine which two churches these could be but with no success. The interpretation has now been given. The first part of the interpretation is this: in my own heart and mind, I had conceived the church that I wanted to minister in, and I had almost convinced myself that God would lead me to this church. One church being shown to me over and over was the church of my own longing and devising. The second church was the reality, that is, the church to which God would eventually lead us. There was, however, a still more significant aspect to the "two churches." The revelation was indicating God was saying, "I will take you where you do not want to go."

When this meaning was given to me, it was the second time that I was told, "God will lead you where you do not want to go." It was simply a prelude to the interpretation of one of the major revelations given to me.

True to his word, God has taken both Joy and me where we did not want to go. True to His word He has always led us back to the central path of our lives and our calling.

These are just a few of the revelations that were given to me.

XXV

COLLINGWOOD

During the days that we lived on Alberta Street we often drove down Forty-first Avenue as far as Kingsway. These are two major thoroughfares in South Vancouver. Sitting inside the corner where these two traffic lanes meet, and just about one-half block off of each, there is a church. It is a fairly large church consisting of the main building and a hall alongside. Forty-first Avenue goes into a long, sweeping curve just as it approaches Kingsway, thus one's attention is turned away from the church. We had seen this church many times, and yet partly because it was set back from the road, partly because it was painted in one rather faded color and partly because shrubs had grown up and covered the signboard, it did not make the kind of impression on the mind that one would hope for. For many months I did not know the name of the church nor to whom it belonged. It turned out to be Collingwood United Church.

The call to Collingwood came in late March, but it was not effective until the first of July. Shortly after receiving the call I made my way into the sanctuary one afternoon and spent about an hour looking the whole building over. There was a beauty in the sanctuary that the exterior did not reveal. I stood in the pulpit, and my gaze was caught by a large room at the back of the church where a balcony would be. It had a glassed-in front and large windows at the back letting in light from the outside. It was a nursery. When I opened the door to go into the room it was evident that it had not been used for two or three years. The rug on the floor and the curtains on the outside windows were mildewed; the walls and ceiling were waterstained from a roof that leaked. The air was oppressive. To myself I said, "This is where we start; we are going to reclaim and revitalize this nursery."

I had been working with a department of the federal government, the Job Creation Branch, that worked with individuals and organizations at creating jobs for the unemployed. In that moment I decided to apply for just such government assistance to begin a total renovation of this church. The government scheme was called the Local Initiative Program. For organizations whose applications were approved the federal government provided salaries, and the employers would take persons off the unemployed rolls, including some hard-to-place persons, and provide the materials needed to do a meaningful piece of work. Not everyone who applied was "funded." But I am ahead of my story. The call to Collingwood was not effective for nearly three months and the next Local Initiative Program was not due to start until the fall of that year.

About four years before this date, while I was still ministering in Gaetz Memorial United Church, it had been revealed to me that I would be moved from Red Deer and that there would be a new church for me. The revelation about the new church showed me that when I saw it I would be perplexed and I would recoil from it. I was shown that I would think the church was dead, but I would take it up in my arms and find not only life in it but also a strength. The church would lay its head upon my breast in trust and response. All of these things happened.

The Local Initiative Grant was applied for and our application was approved. The congregation contributed willingly to provide the materials needed and also funds to purchase a beautiful new rug for the sanctuary. The exterior was completely painted in one main color and two contrasting, colorful trims. Four crosses, one on each side of the tower, were repaired, repainted and then illuminated from behind and with floodlights from above. The total effect has brought great interest and much praise from both the growing congregation and the people of the community.

Once more I am ahead of my story. The people in the Job Creation Branch had become my friends. Many had also placed an interesting trust in me and some had related in an interesting way to "my ministry." Before leaving I said to God in prayer that I would like to do something meaningful to express my gratitude to these people. This prayer was most graciously answered. Many of my fellow workers came with varying requests and almost all received interesting response.

Two other persons left the department on the day that I did. A delightful farewell was held. When the gathering was over one young woman who held a senior executive position remained behind and asked if she could speak with me. She had a physical impairment which she said, "I have had ever since I was three years old." She asked for and received a complete healing.

I have kept in touch with these friends; it remains a happy association.

One question that lingered in my mind in the months after

we had left Red Deer was, "Why did God let us be moved when it appeared to some of us that there was a large group of people who wanted us to stay?"

It seemed to me that in Red Deer there was a wide open door for a great ministry even though there were adversaries.

The answer is now abundantly clear. There is an even greater door for effective service open to us here. There soon began coming to my office many people with many needs. God in His loving kindness blessed many of these people in many ways and in more interesting ways. It is thrilling and beautiful to be a part of all of this.

Nor is this the only part to the explanation. For the first time in our lives we own our own home. It is a beautiful home with a view of ocean, mountain, trees and garden. We live in a beautiful city in a part of the world that is blessed with an excellent climate and many other things.

Nor does this explain it all. You may recall the day that Joy began her work with the new Vancouver company. She felt she was finally settled. I had told her, "You won't be with this company for long."

Her answer, given in a voice of alarm, had been, "Oh, don't tell me that!"

After five months, in early December 1976, Joy tendered her resignation. It was not accepted. She continued her work for one more month. This time she could not be persuaded to remain and left the company at the end of January. Through February we looked for a place for Joy to open her own store. We found it on the first of March, and on the seventeenth of March "Joy's Play and Learn Ltd." opened for business in the field of educational toys and equipment. Joy is reaching out not only to the general public but also to all institutions engaged in the field of early education. We knew this location was not permanent. On October the first of this year we moved into a larger store, in what we feel will be permanent. Joy has an excellent store and is doing well. Our son Brian once more gave us a big assist; so did our daughter, Margaret, and her husband, Doug, and our son David.

When you work with God what looks like the end is often just the beginning.

It was so with us.